FRIGHTFUL
WHEN CHRISTMAS BECAME
DELIGHTFUL

by Dr. Randy T. Johnson

with contributions by:

Noble Baird	John Hubbard
Holly Boston	Eric Jeffrey
Chris Cain	Debbie Kerr
John Carter	Bill Kinney
James Clouse	Josh Lahring
Carole Combs	Chuck Lindsey
Isaiah Combs	James Mann
Jayson Combs	Wes McCullough
Jen Combs	Michelle Moshier
Sierra Combs	Mark O'Connor
Brett Eberle	Jill Osmon
Bryan Fox	Ken Perry
Donna Fox	Philip Piasecki
Michael Fox	Max Sinclair
Debbie Gabbara	Ryan Story
Larry Gabbara	Holly Wells
Danielle Hardenburg	Kyle Wendel
Ben Heddy-Kennedy	Katrina Young
Richie Henson	Tommy Youngquist

Design by: Casey Maxwell

Copyright © 2017 The River Church

All rights reserved. No part of this book may be reproduced or transmitted in any form or by any means, electronic or mechanical, including photocopying, recording or by any information storage and retrieval system, without the written permission of The River Church. Inquiries should be sent to the publisher.

First Edition, October 2017

Published by:
The River Church
8393 E. Holly Rd.
Holly, MI 48442

Scriptures are taken from the Bible,
English Standard Version (ESV)

THE RIVER CHURCH

Printed in the United States of America

CONTENTS

WEEK 1: MARY

Study Guide ... 11
Devotion 1: Greatly Troubled ... 19
Devotion 2: The Favored One ... 21
Devotion 3: How Can It Be? ... 23
Devotion 4: MAGNIFY!...Wait...What? ... 25
Devotion 5: The Powerful Birth Story ... 29
Devotion 6: Treasured ... 31

WEEK 2: JOSEPH

Study Guide ... 35
Devotion 1: It's The Most Wonderful Time Of The Year ... 43
Devotion 2: A Just Man, A Hard Choice ... 45
Devotion 3: Dream Weaver ... 47
Devotion 4: Opportunities In Disguise ... 49
Devotion 5: To Fulfill ... 53
Devotion 6: Obedience — Joseph Or Jonah ... 55

WEEK 3: SHEPHERDS

Study Guide ... 59
Devotion 1: Why Shepherds? ... 69
Devotion 2: Great Fear ... 71
Devotion 3: All People ... 73
Devotion 4: Singing In The Reign ... 75
Devotion 5: Hide Then Go Seek ... 77
Devotion 6: Sweet Tweet ... 79

WEEK 4: FEAR OF THE LORD

Study Guide ... 83
Devotion 1: Autophobia ... 89
Devotion 2: Monophobia ... 91
Devotion 3: Gamophobia ... 93
Devotion 4: Panophobia ... 95
Devotion 5: Nomophobia ... 97
Devotion 6: Thanatophobia ... 99

WEEK 5: HEROD x 24

- Study Guide ... 103
- Devotion 1: Wise Men With Bad News ... 109
- Devotion 2: My Kingdom ... 111
- Devotion 3: Drama King ... 113
- Devotion 4: Liar, Liar, Pants On Fire ... 115
- Devotion 5: Collateral Damage ... 117
- Devotion 6: Death Of A Madman ... 119

WEEK 6: REACH

- Study Guide ... 123
- Devotion 1: Relationship ... 129
- Devotion 2: Moral Law ... 131
- Devotion 3: Three Branches ... 133
- Devotion 4: Got God? ... 135
- Devotion 5: Tax Exempt ... 137
- Devotion 6: Respect ... 139

WEEK 7: GATHER

- Study Guide ... 143
- Devotion 1: Schooling ... 149
- Devotion 2: Equality ... 151
- Devotion 3: People Rule ... 153
- Devotion 4: Ten Commandments ... 155
- Devotion 5: Justice and Morality ... 157
- Devotion 6: Witnesses ... 159

WEEK 8: GROW

- Study Guide ... 163
- Devotion 1: King of Kings ... 169
- Devotion 2: Free Indeed ... 171
- Devotion 3: Creator And Savior ... 173
- Devotion 4: Will Work 4 Food ... 175
- Devotion 5: We Are Family ... 177
- Devotion 6: God's Servant ... 179

WEEK 9: BACK TO REACH

Study Guide	183
Testimony #1	189
Testimony #2	191
Testimony #3	193
Testimony #4	195
Testimony #5	197
Testimony #6	199
Testimony #7	201

FRIGHTFUL
WHEN CHRISTMAS BECAME
DELIGHTFUL

When angels appeared, they would immediately say, **"Do not be afraid!"** Mary, Joseph, and a group of shepherds all met angels and instantly experienced fear. However, that first Christmas their frightful reaction turned into a delightful outcome. Their Savior was born.

Sometimes fear is healthy. The Book of Proverbs repeatedly says, **"The fear of the Lord is the beginning of knowledge."** We need to understand an awe and respect for God, but as believers, we do not need to fear anything else.

Unfortunately, some are too stubborn or self-consumed to appreciate Jesus coming to earth. Herod was one of those who feared losing control. His life went from delightful to living in a frightful state.

Frightful consists of nine study guides for personal or group discussion and fifty-four devotions from Bible passages proclaiming the birth of Jesus and what is a proper response.

01 / *Carole Combs,*
Wife of the Lead Pastor

MARY

Mary

My husband and I usually treat our entire family to a yearly family vacation. Our family has grown through the years from our original seven of us to now twenty-two of us. We have gained wonderful daughter-in-laws, as well as, some of the most amazing grandchildren in the world (sounding a little bias, huh?). One year while we were in Sedona, Arizona, I cannot recall how just my husband and I, our oldest son, Joshua, and his wife, Jennifer, were able to get away for a walk together from the rest of the family. As we were strolling along, Joshua suggested that the four of us walk towards one of the mountains that we could see in the distance. We all agreed to make that trek our destination. Did you know that large objects in the distance appear closer than they really are? After walking a few miles, we all arrived at the foot of the mountain. Joshua had another suggestion. He suggested that we all climb the side of the mountain to the top. I reluctantly said yes (I hadn't learned from the first suggestion). Jen was in her first trimester of her pregnancy, so my husband conveniently declined to do the heroic deed by staying with Jen to guard her against any wild animals. They remained at the foot of the mountain while Joshua and I began to climb the mountain. We found flat enough areas that made it somewhat easy to ascend the mountain. In the ease of the climb, I did not realize how far we had made it off the ground. I looked down, and immediately a great fear came over me. I thought to myself, "What am I doing? Should I stop here and climb back down? Wait a minute; I am afraid of heights!" Joshua was continuing to climb in front of me and above me. He was leading the way, so I continued to follow him. We came to a place on the side of the mountain that had no flat areas to put our feet. The plan was for me to put my foot into Joshua's cupped hands and he would boost me as high as he could. I was to grab a small piece of jagged rock that was sticking out and then pull myself up to the next flat area. My adrenaline was pumping! My whole body was shaking! Success! I have a photo of me on the top of this mountain.

What is one of the scariest things or times you have ever experienced?
___
___
___

I was so delighted that I chose to keep going forward that day. Even though it was very hard, I could have allowed fear to cripple me from experiencing the victory that God brought in my life. I kept remembering Psalm 56:3, **"When I am afraid, I put my trust in you."** Fear is meant for our normal and healthy well-being. However, fear can quickly turn to abnormal and unhealthy. We have turned fear into an everyday part of our existence. We even feel at liberty to share and spread our fear.

When are some times when we have a healthy fear?___
___
___

When are some times when we have an unhealthy fear?___
___
___

Fear is a breeding ground for unbelief and lack of trust. What if when you were a young teenager (or you are now), and an angel came and spoke to you? What if what the angel had to say to you seemed like he surely must have gotten the wrong address? This very event happened to Mary in Luke chapter 1. Mary was a young virgin engaged to be married to a man named Joseph. The angel Gabriel appeared and spoke to Mary. Gabriel began with a hello but went on to tell Mary that she had found favor with God and that God had a purpose for her life. Angel's appearing and speaking to people is not an everyday occurrence now nor was it then.

Luke 1:29 says,

"But she was greatly troubled at the saying, and tried to discern what sort of greeting this might be."

What thoughts do you think were going through Mary's mind? What emotions? _____
_____
_____

Do you think that it might be possible that Mary remembered the readings she had heard as a young child? The prophet Isaiah wrote hundreds of years earlier in Isaiah 7:14, **"Therefore the Lord himself will give you a sign, Behold a virgin shall conceive and bear a son, and shall call his name Immanuel."**

_____
_____
_____

Mary did not have to share verbally her troubled spirit that was going on in her heart and mind; God already knew. **"O Lord, you have searched me and known me! You know when I sit down and when I rise up; you discern my thoughts from afar"** (Psalm 139:1-2). The angel Gabriel told her not to be afraid. God was the God of all comfort then as He still is today. "Yes, Mary, you are the one I have chosen. You are not the richest, you are not the best looking, you are not the most educated, you did not have a perfect life or home, but I have chosen you, do not be afraid!" Mary had nothing to give to God but herself that day. Her favor was from God. It was by His perfect grace. God is calling you as well. He wants to use you for His purpose and His plan here on earth. He is not asking too much from you. You may not feel like you have anything to offer God. He will do the miracles. He will do the equipping. He does the impossible. He just wants to know if you are willing.

Is there something you think God wants you to do now, but you are hesitant? _____
_____
_____

Mary did not let fear cloud up her trust in her God that day. She rose above her greatly troubled feelings. She did not run from the message or the messenger. What if Mary let her emotions control her that day? What if I would have let fear control me while in Sedona? I would have missed out on one of the greatest victories in my life.

Do you recall a time when you let fear rob you of a great experience?
_____
_____
_____

Mary would have missed out on being the vessel for God to use to bring the VICTOR into the world. Jesus was victorious over death, hell, and the grave! Jesus gave you and me victory over defeat! ***"For God gave us a Spirit NOT of fear but of power and love and self-control"*** (2 Timothy 1:7).

How does that verse relate to your life?_____
_____
_____

God expects us to respond as Mary did with the same willingness, obedience, and trust. We can yield to God or resist God. We can go His way or go our way. Embrace what God has for your life. Mary embraced the call of God on her life. It will not exclude some ridicule, some contempt, and maybe some loneliness. It gets lonely sometimes doing right. Mary's faith trusted whatever and wherever

God was leading her. By faith, she knew the Almighty was right there with her now and forever.

Is faith the antonym of fear? Is it the cure? _____
_____
_____

I kept my eyes on my son Joshua and followed him as he climbed higher and higher. Before I knew it, we were at the top. Jesus wants to take you above the circumstances around you. However, most of us would rather hold onto the fear and stay in our circumstances. We would rather be in control of the situation instead of giving God the control. All this does is crush your faith and trust in the Lord. Obedience is what God asks of you. Fear will cause you to disobey God. I know some of you understand because it was me at one time in my life. You have to see it all planned out in black and white before you will make a step of obedience to God. It has to all add up and make sense to you.

It did not make sense that a young virgin would give birth to any child, and not the Son of the Most High. Mary allowed delight in the things of God to replace fright! She believed when it was humanly impossible. **"For NOTHING will be impossible with God"** (Luke 1:37). Step out of your comfort zone. This zone only has fear, faithlessness, and mistrust in God. Allow the grace of God to lead you into God's perfect purpose for your life. God has a lot of mountains, and every mountain surely will look different than mine.

Romans 8:31 summarizes this topic so well, "What then shall we say to these things? If God is for us, who can be against us?"

Mary

What giant, struggle, or fear do you need to conquer? _____
_____
_____

What mountain or challenge do you need to approach? _____
_____
_____

Mary / Devotion 1

GREATLY TROUBLED

Debbie Kerr / *Office Administrator*

Can you think of a time you received a phone call or an email that instantly incited anxiety, confusion, fear, and doubt? I remember the night four years ago when I was home alone in the early evening, and my phone rang. A ringing phone is not usually a fearful event unless you are expecting unsettling news, which I was not. I was unprepared for the news I was about to hear. My sister's trembling voice was on the other end of the phone, and I heard the dreaded words, "Debbie, Dad is gone!" Immediately, I was in a state of denial and thought, "there must be a mistake, I just talked to him the other day, and he sounded fine." The next voice I heard was a man I did not know. My sister had handed the phone to a police officer who confirmed and offered his condolences in six of the most painful words I have ever heard, "I'm sorry for your loss, Ma'am." My state of denial quickly became my reality. Instantly, I was flooded with all kinds of emotions, first and foremost being grief and sorrow, followed by immense fear, anxiety, and uncertainty. I guess I would sum up those five emotions into one word, TROUBLED! The news instantly sent my mind whirling in many directions. The main concern was who is going to care for my sweet mother who could not be left alone for more than a few minutes due to Alzheimer's disease. God quickly calmed my fears and proved Himself faithful by going before us and having things and people in place. God was very near to us during that time just as He promised in His word, **"The Lord is near to the brokenhearted and saves the crushed in Spirit"** (Psalm 34:18).

I cannot even begin to imagine what a young virgin girl must have felt when the Angel of the Lord visited her one day with some of the most incredible yet terrifying and definitely unexpected news imaginable. In Luke 1:28-29 we read, **"'Greetings, O favored one, the Lord is with you!' But she was greatly troubled at the saying, and tried to discern what sort of greeting this might be."** My first thought is, greatly troubled....Ummm, NO KIDDING! If an Angel of the Lord visited me with an important sacred message, I might be slightly worse off than troubled. Mary, a young teenage virgin girl, was just told that she was going to bear a son, not just any son but the Son of the Most High! Ok, right there I would have freaked out! I would have gone on Facebook, and my status would have been labeled, Feeling Freaked Out along with the big eyes emoticon. What in the world?!?!? How can this be? What will I tell my parents, what will I tell Joseph, my betrothed? How will I ever show my face in public because who is going to believe I have not done something terrible! These are all the things I would have been thinking.

Mary feeling troubled is completely understandable and appropriate. I am sure the initial shock and days proceeding were unsettling for sure, but God was with her just like He was with me when I faced trouble. Throughout Scripture we see God going before His people and preparing the way. God never fails to deliver on His promise to provide all that we need when we cast our cares on Him. He freely gives us a peace that passes all understanding. How awesome for Mary to be **"Highly favored of God!"** What an honor and privilege to be the one chosen to carry our Savior in her young womb. He turned her trouble into triumph!

Jesus said in John 14:1, **"Let not your hearts be troubled. Believe in God believe also in me."** God wants all of His children to trust Him at all times but especially in times of trouble and great distress. Remember, His ways are perfect. He has a purpose and a plan and will provide everything that we need. He will work all things together for good to those who love Him and are the called according to His purpose (Romans 8:28).

Mary / Devotion 2

THE FAVORED ONE

Donna Fox / *Assistant to the Growth Pastor*

"*And the angel said to her, 'Do not be afraid, Mary, for you have found favor with God.'*" (Luke 1:30)

"I have found favor with you." Would we not all love to hear those words from our God? What an honor, to have God find favor with you! It ranks right up there with **"Well done, good and faithful servant"** (Matthew 25:21).

Such was the case with Mary. She was maybe 14 years old. In that culture, girls were betrothed (engaged) at a young age. Mary was betrothed to Joseph but was not yet married. An angel appeared to Mary and told her she had found favor with God and would have a baby. Imagine what she must have been thinking when she heard those words. "Get outta here" or "You are joking," is what we might say today.

How does one "find favor with God?" Is this something we can earn by good works, or buy? Is it something we can steal away from another? No. It is a result of our faith. We are all unclean, sinners, fallen from grace (Isaiah 64:6). But Mary was pleasing, approved, liked by God, and chosen to carry our Lord and Savior in her womb. She was a virgin, so what would Joseph say? What would others think? They surely would not hear the news and say "Congratulations, Mary, you are carrying God's Son and it is a miracle." No, they would likely say, "You liar, you whore." They would see her as a very immoral person.

The angel told Mary the child would be named Jesus. **"And behold, you will conceive in your womb and bear a son, and you shall call his name Jesus"** (Luke 1:31). Mary was the first person ever to hear the name of Jesus. What an honor! Do you think she comprehended what this all meant? I doubt it. She knew she was specially chosen, for sure. She believed in God and trusted His plan for her life. But still, it could not have been easy. No one would believe her. She had to remain strong in her faith and trust that God would work out the details, which He did!

Mary's cousin, Elizabeth, had a similar experience. Her husband, Zacharias, and she were not able to have children. They were aged when Zacharias was visited by an angel, similar to Mary, to announce that Elizabeth would bear a son and his name would be John (Luke 1:13). Fast forward six months later to Mary. We do not know if Mary knew about Elizabeth at the time, but she inevitably found out shortly when she visited Elizabeth and the unborn baby, John, leaped in his mother's womb! How exciting to have a family member to share her joy with, because undoubtedly everyone else was looking down on Mary.

Another person in the Bible who found favor in God's sight was Noah. **"But Noah found favor in the eyes of the Lord"** (Genesis 6:8). He was used in a mighty way to save his family and the animals during the great flood. God chose Noah for a particular purpose because of his faith.

God chose Mary, Elizabeth, Noah, and others because of their great faith. We need to strive to have this great faith so that God will use each of us for His will and in His timing.

Mary / Devotion 3

HOW CAN IT BE?

Debbie Gabbara / *Assistant to the Gathering Pastor*

"Behold, the virgin shall conceive and bear a son, and they shall call his name Immanuel (which means, 'God with us')." Matthew 1:23

"And Mary said, 'Behold, I am the servant of the Lord; let it be to me according to your word.' And the angel departed from her." Luke 1:38

Mary sat alone thinking to herself, "How can it be? Was he really an angel? Am I really going to have a baby? How can it be? I have never known a man, yet, I believe that nothing is impossible with God. I know His Word is true. He has done great and mighty things. But, why me? I am an ordinary girl. How can it be?"

That was months ago, and now she was great with child. As they made their way toward Bethlehem, Mary's mind wandered, "I am so far from home. Where will I deliver the child? He is not just a child; this baby is the Son of God. How can it be?"

There was no room in the inn, but the innkeeper allowed her and Joseph to stay in the stable. There, Mary delivered her baby. As the angel had instructed, they would call him JESUS. Mary whispered his name, "Jesus" as she looked into His beautiful face. He was extraordinary, He was her child, yet the angel said, **"He would be great and would be called the Son of the Most High."** And, **"the child to be born will be called holy - the Son of God."** I am just a girl; how can it be?

The shepherds came in the night. An angel told them where to find the baby who would be swaddled in cloths and lying in a manger. They said there was a multitude of heavenly hosts praising God and saying, **"'Glory to God in the highest, and on earth peace among those with whom he is pleased!' Mary treasured all these things and pondered them in her heart."** She wondered still, how can it be?

Mary held her sweet baby and remembered her prayer, **"My soul magnifies the Lord, and my spirit rejoices in God my Savior, for he has looked on the humble estate of his servant."** She whispered in her heart, "I am your servant, and you are God! That is how it can be!"

> *"For to us a child is born, to us a son is given; and the government shall be upon his shoulder, and his name shall be called Wonderful Counselor, Mighty God, Everlasting Father, Prince of Peace."* Isaiah 9:6

Mary / Devotion 4

MAGNIFY! ...
WAIT ... WHAT?

Holly Wells / *Assistant to Pastor Jim*

When was the last time an angel appeared before you and prophesied over your life? Yeah, me neither. It has never happened. But, imagine for a moment that it has. Imagine this: you are in your early teens, going about a simple life, after all, you live in a peasant's town in a poor area. You are pretty common, plain, and unassuming, and you are engaged to a working-class fiancé, a carpenter. One day as you are going about your business, an angel appears before you and says that you are favored and that **"the Lord is with you"** (Luke 1:28). Just at that mere greeting, I think I would have instantly passed out! You? Although Mary thankfully kept it together, the Bible says she was **"greatly troubled"** and tried to figure out what this meant (verse 29). Gabriel told her not to be afraid because, with this favor from God, she would conceive and bear a son named Jesus. He told her that He would be great; He would **"be called the Son of the Most High"** (verse 32). Gabriel told this young Jewish girl that her Son would be given the throne of David, He would reign over the house of Jacob forever, and there would be no end to His kingdom. (Now, if I was somehow still coherent at this point, I am confident I would not be able to speak let alone begin dialoguing as Mary did with Gabriel.) He continued to share how it would all happen, about how she would be the mother to the Son of God. This was f-a-r from an ordinary day!

What would have been your response? Maybe one of shock and disbelief? What about worrying how your reputation would be ruined when word got out of this unexplainable pregnancy since you are engaged? How would you explain this to your fiancé?

Would you fret that "this was not a part of the plan!" I believe Mary's response reflected the exact reason she was chosen, **"Behold, I am the servant of the Lord; let it be to me according to your word"** (verse 38).

Mary soon traveled to visit her relative Elizabeth, who was pregnant with John (as in the Baptist) and when Elizabeth heard Mary's greeting as she came into her house, the baby leaped in Elizabeth's womb, and she was filled with the Holy Spirit. Elizabeth knew at that moment that Mary was the mother of the Lord (verse 39-45). And Mary's response? It was not one of gossip or recounting the details of her encounter with the angel Gabriel. It was not filled with "what if...," "why...," or "how come?" Mary's response was yet again one that was firmly anchored in the Lord. Mary's response was a song of praise.

Luke 1:46-55 is referred to as 'The Magnificat' which is the Latin word for 'magnifies.' Mary's soul magnified the Lord and rejoiced in God, her Savior. As I read through this section, a few things stood out. First, notice that Mary knew the Lord before the angel appeared to her. The relationship she had with the Lord was the reason He chose her for something great, to become the mother of the Messiah, Jesus Christ. And though Mary was most extraordinary, we must also be careful not to elevate her beyond what Scripture teaches. She was human, a woman who was a recipient of God's blessing, but she is not who we appeal to for blessing. 1 Timothy 2:5-6 states, **"For there is one God and one Mediator between God and men, the man Christ Jesus, who gave Himself as a ransom for all."** Mary fully knew this. Next, because her heart and mind were already saturated with the Word of God, she submitted herself unconditionally to the Lord without worry of her reputation or fret of the future (verse 38). Rather, she instantly and humbly praised Him for His glory and majesty. Because Mary intimately knew God as her Savior, she was able to rejoice in His holiness and faithfulness, glory, and strength. She worshiped Him for His mercy and power while taking no credit for anything good in herself. Mary joyfully confessed God as the one who did great things for her.

Let us be exhorted and encouraged through Mary's example by taking personal inventory. Are your mind and heart continually being saturated with the Word of God? How is your relationship with Him growing 'daily' so that you may know the Lord and experience a sweet intimacy with Him like no other? What is your response when He calls you to something greater or something crazy that may tarnish your reputation? What is the song in your heart? How do you magnify the Lord?

Mary / Devotion 5

THE POWERFUL BIRTH STORY

Chris Cain

Have you ever noticed that when you are in the presence of a group of women, and one of them is pregnant, the bulk of the conversation surrounds one's birth experience? Details of due dates, choice of hospital, the method of induction, labor, and dilation are just some of the topics and stories being shared. Some women will write down their birth story, while others will blog or scrapbook all about the experience.

I was asked to contribute to this book just two days after my third grandchild was born. My son and daughter-in-law had just experienced first-hand, one of life's most powerful experiences. It is a memory they have captured and will tell for many years to come.

> Luke 2:1-7 says, *"In those days a decree went out from Caesar Augustus that all the world should be registered. This was the first registration when Quirinius was governor of Syria. And all went to be registered, each to his own town. And Joseph also went up from Galilee, from the town of Nazareth, to Judea, to the city of David, which is called Bethlehem, because he was of the house and lineage of David, to be registered with Mary, his betrothed, who was with child. And while they were there, the time came for her to give birth. And she gave birth to her firstborn son and wrapped him in swaddling cloths and laid him in a manger, because there was no place for them in the inn."*

I read Luke 2:1-7 in several different Bible translations and most translations have titled this passage as, "The Birth of Christ" yet there were not many facts that made it much of a story. I wanted details. How did pregnant Mary survive the 60 plus mile donkey ride? Did her water break? How long did she labor? Luke does not awe us with stories of booming fireworks in the sky and does not make mention of God's mighty hand at work. Instead, he seems to share more on the Emperor and the governor of Syria. It is basically the powerful showing off their power while Joseph and Mary appear to be left quite powerless. But let us not miss the significance and power of Luke's account. What we think is a frightful and sad birth story is truly a delightful and humble circumstance of God's powerful redemption plan.

> John 3:16 says, *"For God so loved the world, that He gave His only Son, that whoever believes in Him should not perish but have eternal life."*
>
> John 1:12-13 adds, *"But to all who did receive Him, who believed in His name, he gave the right to become children of God, who were born, not of blood nor of the will of the flesh nor of the will of man, but of God."*

If you have been born again, you have a birth story to share. Do not underestimate the power of your story that can point people to God's bigger story; the story of the Gospel of Christ which is the greatest and most powerful story ever told.

Mary / Devotion 6

TREASURED

Sierra Combs / *Women's Ministry Director*

My dear mother is extremely sentimental. Growing up, her motto was always, "Let's make a memory!" It did not matter how grand or basic the moment, she wanted to remember it. It was silly to me then, but now that I have my children, I get it. I too want to savor every precious second with my family, taking mental pictures and storing them up in my memory bank. I vividly remember my first Christmas as a mother, with the sweetest baby boy in my arms and overflowing joy in my heart! I TREASURE those moments. I relive them in my head over and over because I never want to forget them.

It seems I am not the first to cling dearly to precious Christmas memories; it has been happening to mothers everywhere since the very first Christmas, starting with the mother of Jesus herself. Luke 2:8-19 tells us about some local shepherds watching over their sheep in nearby fields when they are suddenly visited by an angel, bringing **"good news of great joy that will be for all the people."** And if that was not enough, they were then joined by a whole crew of angels **"praising God, and saying 'Glory to God in the highest!'"** They could not contain their excitement and ran to town to find their Messiah, a baby wrapped in swaddling clothes, and lying in a manger. **"And when they saw it, they made known the saying that had been told them concerning this child. And all who heard it wondered at what the shepherds told them. But Mary treasured up all these things, pondering them in her heart."**

If there was ever anything that should be treasured, it was this! What a whirlwind everything must have been for Mary! A young unmarried Jewish girl living an ordinary life until an angel appears and tells her that God has chosen her to carry and give birth to the Messiah. She immediately submits to God's plan, despite the scandal of it all, despite having no idea of the future. She delivers her baby, the King of Kings, God in the flesh, and lays Him in a manger. But Mary did not just treasure everything that had happened. Verse 19 says she also **"pondered them in her heart."** She thought about them. She stored them away in her inmost being. While the shepherds were excitedly telling everyone in town about the new Messiah, Mary quietly treasured and pondered everything she had seen and heard, remembering and reliving every detail that she could. Little did she know how important this would be. Soon there would be a time where her Son would not be lying safe and snug in her arms. Soon she would see Him ridiculed, mocked, beaten, and bruised. Soon she would see the absolute worst thing a mother could ever see, her precious Son hanging on a cross, dying for her sins and the sins of the world. It would be in those times that she would need to pull out those treasured thoughts she had stored in her heart. She would need to remember the words of the angel when he told her that her Son **"will be great and will be called the Son of the Most High" and that "the Lord God will give to him the throne of his father David, and he will reign over the house of Jacob forever, and of his kingdom there will be no end"** (Luke 1:32-33). She would need to remember that the God who miraculously made her a mother was a God who keeps His promises. He is so faithful. That is surely something to be treasured!

02 / *Philip Piasecki,*
Worship Leader

JOSEPH

Joseph

When we think of Christmas, most of us think of a joyful time in our lives. We think back to different Christmas mornings growing up, remembering certain gifts and special memories with friends and family. We have traditions that we did with our parents, and now we carry those on with our children. It is a magical time. Personally, I have so many different great memories of Christmas. I remember getting my Nintendo 64 with Zelda, getting a shotgun the year I turned 13, and getting Detroit Pistons tickets when they were actually good! One particular tradition that Mary and I are carrying on within our family is always reading the Christmas story before any presents are touched. We know that Christmas is first and foremost about Christ, and this is a perfect way to keep that whole morning in focus. My most precious Christmas memories are reading that story every Christmas morning.

What are some of your favorite Christmas memories or traditions?
_____
_____
_____

What is the best gift you have ever given and received?
_____
_____
_____

One part of the Christmas story that commonly seems to get overlooked is Joseph's story. The buildup to that first Christmas must have been terrifying at times for Joseph. He was betrothed to Mary, and then he finds out that she is pregnant. That news would have rocked his entire world. He was an honorable man, planning on taking Mary as his wife, and then Mary tells him that news. We know from Scripture that when Mary told him, Joseph decided that he would quietly divorce her. We better understand how gracious this decision was when we look at the Law in Deuteronomy and see what other action he could have legally taken.

> Deuteronomy 22:23-24 says, *"If there is a betrothed virgin, and a man meets her in the city and lies with her, then you shall bring them both out to the gate of that city, and you shall stone them to death with stones, the young woman because she did not cry for help though she was in the city, and the man because he violated his neighbor's wife. So you shall purge the evil from your midst."*

Put yourself in Joseph's shoes, what would your reaction have been to the news of Mary's pregnancy? _____

_____

_____

> Matthew 1:19-20 says, *"And her husband Joseph, being a just man and unwilling to put her to shame, resolved to divorce her quietly. But as he considered these things, behold, an angel of the Lord appeared to him in a dream, saying, 'Joseph, son of David, do not fear to take Mary as your wife, for that which is conceived in her is from the Holy Spirit.'"*

> Matthew 1:24-25 adds, *"When Joseph woke from sleep, he did as the angel of the Lord commanded him: he took his wife, but knew her not until she had given birth to a son. And he called his name Jesus."*

What would your reaction have been to hearing this news from the Angel if you were Joseph? _____

_____

_____

We see that Joseph justifiably could have had Mary stoned, but instead he decided to just divorce her quietly so she would not be shamed. Then the Angel of the Lord appears to him and validates Mary's story. Scripture tells us that he did as the Angel of the Lord commanded. We meet Joseph in Scripture as he is having his whole life turned upside down. He was a carpenter, planning on marrying a girl and living a quiet life, and instead, finds out she is going to give birth to the Savior of the world. I think it is safe to assume Mary and Joseph are now the gossips of the town. Mary is pregnant before marriage AND Joseph decides to still marry her. However, Joseph trusted God and did what was right in God's eyes. He did not let the concern of what the worldly consequences of his decision would be. He would have known the reactions and the repercussions of his decision, yet he followed the command of the Angel.

Would you have struggled to follow the command of the Angel?

_____

_____

_____

So when we look at this story, how can we apply it to our lives? Joseph did not let the fear of persecution from the world stop him from doing what Christ had commanded. This is something that we all experience each day. We have to decide daily if we are going to do what Christ has commanded us, even though it may cost us something. We may lose friends, lose jobs, or even lose our life, but following Christ is better than all those things.

Do you struggle doing what is right because of fear of persecution?

_____

_____

_____

> 1 Peter 3:14 says, *"But even if you should suffer for righteousness' sake, you will be blessed. Have no fear of them, nor be troubled."*
>
> Romans 5:3-5 adds, *"Not only that, but we rejoice in our sufferings, knowing that suffering produces endurance, and endurance produces character, and character produces hope, and hope does not put us to shame, because God's love has been poured into our hearts through the Holy Spirit who has been given to us."*

How do these verses encourage you in your walk with Christ?

_____
_____
_____

There are going to be times in each of our lives where we have to decide between pleasing the world and pleasing Christ. Let us get more specific about "the world." There are going to be times when we have to decide between pleasing our friends, family, bosses, and co-workers and pleasing Christ. Thinking of it in those terms makes it a lot more personal.

Can you think of a time you had to choose between Christ and the people listed above? _____

_____
_____

Scripture encourages us that if we suffer for righteousness sake, we will be blessed. Romans shows us the fruit that suffering produces in our lives. We were not meant to live comfortable lives that never bring us persecution. If we are living a life that proclaims Christ, we will experience persecution and hardship. Acts 5:17-42 is a story of the Apostles being arrested for preaching Jesus. Look at the incredible example they leave for us in the Scriptures.

> Acts 5:40-42 says, *"And when they had called in the apostles, they beat them and charged them not to speak in the name of Jesus, and let them go. Then they left the presence of the council, rejoicing that they were counted worthy to suffer dishonor for the name. And every day, in the temple and from house to house, they did not cease teaching and preaching that the Christ is Jesus."*

The apostles rejoiced that they were counted worthy to suffer for the name of Jesus. Reading this passage brings tears to my eyes. They were beaten, released, and they continued to preach about Jesus anyways. Many of us are too afraid to tell friends and family about Jesus because we think they may get annoyed with us. Many of us are too afraid to follow the commands of Christ when we are on the job because we are worried about getting fired. We cannot let fear keep us from living the life that Christ requires of us. I am sure Joseph was terrified to take Mary as his wife. The social implications are too many to number. Imagine if he had let that fear keep him from listening to the command of Christ. He would have missed out on being the earthly father of the Savior of the world!

What are some things you could miss out on if you do not live your life fully for Christ? _____
_____
_____

In what ways are you going to start living more boldly for Christ?
_____
_____
_____

We need to hear the commands of Christ and follow them no matter the cost. Being obedient to God is worth more than anything this world has to offer. That first Christmas was terrifying for Joseph, but he understood that he could not let the fear of persecution stop him from following the commands of God.

Joseph / Devotion 1

"IT'S THE MOST WONDERFUL TIME OF THE YEAR"

Katrina Young / *Nursery and Pre-K Director*

Christmas has always been my favorite time of the year. Our family always got together and celebrated even when there were struggles, pain, and hardships in our lives. My mom was the most enthusiastic about Christmas, and nothing was going to steal her joy. She would always say to us, "Whatever it is, it will wait until tomorrow, tomorrow it will look different and then you can decide how to handle it." Whatever the crisis was, big or small, it had to wait. I did not realize the wisdom in her words then, but now I cherish them.

When I read the story of Jesus' birth and that very first Christmas, I have to wonder what Joseph must have been experiencing. What he had planned for his life had now taken a drastic turn, the woman that he is betrothed to was "....with child from the Holy Spirit." At a time when they must have been planning their wedding ceremony, he is now faced with making a decision while in the midst of a crisis that he did not see coming. Joseph gives us a perfect example of what to do in an impossible situation. He pondered his decision, and he listened to the direction that was given by the angel sent by God; little did he know that God had something better in mind.

Matthew 1:22-23 says, *"All this took place to fulfill what the Lord had said through the prophet: 'Behold! The virgin will be with child and will give birth to a son, and they will call him Immanuel' — which means, 'God with us.'"*

We are all faced with life changes that we did not expect, things happen that are not within our plan, and we have to decide how to move forward. Joseph and Mary were right in what seemed to be an impossible situation. Proverbs 3:5-6 says, **"Trust in the Lord with all your heart, and do not lean on your own understanding. In all your ways acknowledge him, and he will make straight your paths."** Both Mary and Joseph questioned what they could not explain but trusted God and found themselves in the middle of His plan and the fulfillment of prophecy. They were entrusted with the very first Christmas gift, the birth of our Savior.

Whatever the circumstances life has thrown at you this Christmas, ponder and wait on direction from your Heavenly Father, the greatest present to receive is 'His Presence.'

> Romans 8:28 says, *"And we know that for those who love God all things work together for good, for those who are called according to his purpose."*

Joseph / Devotion 2

A JUST MAN
A HARD CHOICE

Bryan Fox / *Deacon of Facilities*

Back in Joseph and Mary's day, to become married, there were two steps. First, came the betrothal which was actually the legal part and was a covenant. Since vows were spoken, it was binding until death do they part. Usually, it was done with the payment of a bride price and witnessed by two people, and the reciting of the traditional vows, "Thou art consecrated to me according to the law of Moses and of Israel."

According to the customs, the bride and groom would live separately for one year, in their own parents' homes. This was to maintain the purity of the woman. If she were to become pregnant during that year, she was not pure, the marriage could be annulled, and the woman could be stoned to death. If she were pure after the year, the wedding ceremony would take place after which the marriage would be consummated.

Now Joseph had a problem. Being of the house of David, how could he as a "righteous" man be married to someone who obviously had sinned and betrayed their covenant? Matthew 1:19 says, **"And her husband Joseph, being a just man and unwilling to put her to shame, resolved to divorce her quietly."** He must have been deeply hurt and betrayed, but also must have loved her dearly. He did not choose to seek revenge or disgrace her by bringing her in front of the judge to determine her fate. He showed his godly character by being respectful to her in his decision.

God is no different now than He was in biblical days. He knows the whole story, knows how things will turn out in the end, and He knows how you will get there. I often think about a sermon Pastor Jim preached using the illustration of God working upstream, He knows all, even when you have no clue what to do or how to approach a problem. It helps to know that no matter what you are going through, we need to rely on His perfect will and trust in Him to lead us on the right path with all of our decisions. Study God's Word, earnestly ask for His will to be revealed to you through prayer and seek godly counsel so your decision can be pleasing and be honoring to God.

Joseph / Devotion 3

DREAM WEAVER

Ken Perry / *Assistant to the Reach Pastor*

Do you remember your dreams? I do not. I sometimes remember that I had a dream and remembered whether they were funny or sad, but I rarely, if ever, remember the content. I am not sure whether it is a blessing not to remember, but I am glad I do not have to decide what or even if they mean something. We can read many things into our dreams. Some are good, some bad, and most mean nothing, but there have been careers built in modern psychology based on the interpretation of someone's dreams.

God used dreams to communicate many times in the Bible. We read of Daniel being called in to interpret King Nebuchadnezzar's dream in Daniel chapter 2. Genesis 40 and 41 relate times when Joseph interpreted Pharaoh's dreams, and it was instrumental in elevating him to the second highest position in Egypt. The position was later used to save Israelites and Egyptians from a horrible famine. Solomon and even Pontius Pilate's wife were communicated to through dreams.

To the point, I wonder what it might have looked like had God not come to Joseph in a dream? Think for a moment that these words might not have been written by Matthew in the first chapter, **"But as he considered these things, behold, an angel of the Lord appeared to him in a dream, saying, 'Joseph, son of David, do not fear to take Mary as your wife, for that which is conceived in her is from the Holy Spirit'"** (verse 20). Benson's commentary describes it this way, "while he was deliberating with himself, <u>and in danger of innocently doing wrong</u>, the angel of the Lord appeared unto him." Joseph was already trying to do the right thing. He was weighing his options to protect both himself and the reputation of Mary. He had not made anything public, yet the Lord saw his heart and spoke to him in a way that would certainly have had the most impact on him.

I wonder how many times the Lord has kept you and I, while trying to do good, from innocently doing wrong? How often has He, in His all-knowing ways, made provision for a better option through means that can only come from the one who is intimately concerned with the hearts and reputations of good men and women?

Spend some time giving thanks and adoration to Him. Realize His primary means of communication to His people is through His word, as 2 Timothy 3:16-17 says, **"All Scripture is God-breathed and is useful for teaching, rebuking, correcting and training in righteousness, so that the man of God may be thoroughly equipped for every good work."** However, we need to be open to any way He chooses to reveal His will to us, yet we need to carefully check any such guidance we receive with Scripture and godly counsel to be sure it is from the Lord. Anything which contradicts Scripture is not from God. Our minds and even Satan are capable of producing great deception in such subjective areas. Just do not mistake every bad dream as a sign that God is disappointed with you. It just might be a bad pumpkin spice latte from the night before.

Joseph / Devotion 4

OPPORTUNITIES IN DISGUISE

Holly Boston / *Women's Ministry Director*

As a parent of young adults, I occasionally look back and wish I had handled things differently. When my children were very young, their toys were inexpensive, and Santa was overly generous. Big mistake! As my children got older, their "toys" became quite expensive, and the conversation sounded like this: "Santa cannot afford all of that. What do you want your big gift to be?" After I had received Christ as my Savior, the conversation began to change as well as how we celebrated Christmas. We still talked about "your one big gift," but we now realized it was Jesus. Free commercial: Parents, start with the proper focus, because it becomes very difficult to remove the world from their focus as they get older.

When I was asked to write about Joseph's Christmas and how it went from frightful to delightful, my focus immediately went to wondering about his "big gift." See how that worldly focus sticks with you? Obviously, Joseph's big gift was Jesus! Or could there have been one before his Son even arrived?

> Matthew 1:18-21 says, **"Now the birth of Jesus Christ took place in this way. When his mother Mary had been betrothed to Joseph, before they came together she was found with child from the Holy Spirit. And her husband Joseph, being a just man and unwilling to put her to shame, resolved to divorce her quietly. But as he considered these things, behold, an angel of the Lord appeared to him in a dream, saying, 'Joseph, son of David, do not fear to take Mary as your wife, for that which is conceived in her is from the Holy Spirit. She will bear a son,**

and you shall call his name Jesus, for he will save his people from their sins.'"

I believe we see Joseph's first big Christmas present in verse 21, **"And you shall call his name Jesus."** God was giving Joseph the opportunity to be part of His plan to save the world and to experience the love, power, provision, and protection of the One True Living God. Joseph is at a crossroads in his life. What if Joseph had chosen to oppose God's plan? Who would blame him? One day he has his whole life planned and the next it appears his world is burning down around him. Have you ever been there? Imagine the pain, fear, anger, disappointment, and betrayal he must have felt after learning of Mary's condition. We see Joseph presented with an opportunity disguised as a raging storm with unbearable circumstances.

As I thought about this opportunity, I could not help but think of Isaiah 55:8, **"For my thoughts are not your thoughts, neither are your ways my ways, declares the LORD."** Throughout the Bible, we see these opportunities in disguise. Each person was faced with a choice between opportunity and opposition. Abraham's opportunity required him to leave everything he knew for the unknown. Moses' opportunity required him to go up against Pharaoh despite overwhelming doubts and fears. Gideon was faced with leading his people into battle against seemingly insurmountable odds. Joseph, like many before him, chose opportunity. He chose to rest on and believe in the Word of God despite overwhelming circumstances.

As I write this, I find myself at my crossroads. I see circumstances in my life that seem insurmountable. I am faced with the decision to oppose God's plan for my life or to view it as an opportunity to experience God. Up until now, I have spent more time in opposition (in my heart) than I care to admit. Today, through the power and strength of the Holy Spirit, I choose opportunity. What will you choose?

John MacArthur said, "If you look at God through your circumstances, He will seem small and very far away, but if by faith you look at your circumstances through God, He will draw very near and reveal His greatness to you."

Joseph / Devotion 5

TO FULFILL

Michael Fox / *Creative Director*

We have been studying in our current series: Frightful, When Christmas became Delightful. When I attempt to put myself in Joseph's shoes during this time, I can see both emotions in "Joseph's Christmas," both frightful and delightful. We were told in Isaiah 7:14, **"Therefore the Lord himself will give you a sign. Behold, the virgin shall conceive and bear a son, and shall call his name Immanuel."**

I can imagine that on the day Joseph found out that Mary was with child, there were some frightful emotions in his life. Matthew 1:18 says, **"Now the birth of Jesus Christ took place in this way. When his mother Mary had been betrothed to Joseph, before they came together she was found to be with child from the Holy Spirit."**

There may have been a few things he was frightened about: What would everyone think when they found out? Joseph was not married to Mary at the time. Who is the father of the child? I would imagine Joseph knew it was not his child, and I could imagine the emotions that go along with that as well. We have all had times in our lives where we have been frightened. Obviously, this would be a big one! Christmas is a time that brings out lots of emotions, and it is easy to get caught up and be frightened. Do I have enough money to provide my family Christmas presents? Am I able to spend enough time with my family this Christmas? Will my children be happy with the presents I bought them?

If we look back to Joseph's Christmas, we can have comfort in knowing the real meaning of Christmas. This time in Joseph's life, while very frightful in the beginning, quickly turned to delightful! When we start with the foundation and focus on Christ, any issue we have can eventually turn delightful. Joseph quickly found out the reason why his fiancé was with child, Matthew 1:20 says, **"But as he considered these things, behold, an angel of the Lord appeared to him in a dream, saying, 'Joseph, son of David, do not fear to take Mary as your wife, for that which is conceived in her is from the Holy Spirit.'"** and in verse 22 continues, **"All this took place to fulfill what the Lord had spoken by the prophet."** This happened to Joseph ultimately to fulfill God's plan. God has a plan for each one of our lives, and even though sometimes it seems frightful as we go through it, if we learn to lean on God to fulfill His plan for our lives, it can quickly become delightful! Joseph was frightened because he saw what made sense to him, but only when he turned to God, God was able to reveal His plan, and He was able to turn that fright into delight.

Joseph / Devotion 6

OBEDIENCE – JOSEPH OR JONAH?

Jill Osmon / *Assistant to Lead Pastor*

"When Joseph woke from sleep, he did as the angel of the Lord commanded him: he took his wife, but knew her not until she had given birth to a son. And he called his name Jesus." Matthew 1:24-25

We have been looking at Joseph all week, and we end with his obedience. He found himself in an impossible situation; a difficult decision needed to be made. I am sure as he was looking at the options, he believed he chose the best possible path that both helped and protected Mary and removed himself from it. God had other plans.

God had other plans. It can be terrifying coming to that realization, it can be freeing coming to that realization, but that realization always means stepping out in faith. What do we do when we are faced with difficult situations? Do we listen to God? Do we try and make it go away with a nice little bow? Joseph, when faced with a command from God, chose to listen, even though it was difficult, even though it meant a monumental change to his life, he obeyed. He obeyed, not begrudgingly, but with reverence and honor toward God. Obedience can be ridiculously difficult, even for someone like me who is a rule follower, I still find it difficult to be obedient when it is uncomfortable or means doing something, quite frankly, I do not want to do.

I always think of Jonah when I think of obedience. In Jonah 1:1-2, God told Jonah to go to Ninevah, **"Now the word of the Lord came to Jonah the son of Amittai, saying, 'Arise, go to Nineveh,**

that great city, and call out against it, for their evil has come up before me.'" You continue to read, and you see that Jonah flees and goes far away from Nineveh. Knowing the whole story, seeing God's redemption and Jonah's inevitable obedience, makes me shake my head when Jonah flees multiple times and finds himself in the belly of a large fish. Why did he not just obey the first time? He knows God is sovereign, he knows God's plan will overcome, yet he ran because he did not want to be uncomfortable. Can we be honest right now? Most of the time we are Jonah, not Joseph. We fight God's will, we fight His commands, and then we are shocked to find ourselves in the belly of a large fish. See the difference between Jonah and Joseph is not disobedience versus obedience. Instead, it is how obedience with a humble and worshipful heart can change you, allow you to experience a life only the Creator of the Universe can provide.

If you keep reading Jonah's story, you see that he obeys, and he gets to witness God rescue people that were headed toward destruction. Jonah 3:5 says, **"And the people of Nineveh believed God."** God allowed Jonah to be the tool that brought thousands to the saving grace of God, yet Jonah was annoyed with God for using him. He knew God could have rescued them without him; he could have stayed in his comfortable life, without taking any risks. How many times do we see God's amazing work and we get annoyed because it is inconvenient and uncomfortable for us? Joseph, however, obeyed, with joy and although he still had a difficult road, it was a road full of God's love, grace, glory, and His Son. It was difficult and uncomfortable, but Joseph recognized the unimaginable honor to be used by God. So, how will you obey? Will you be a Jonah or a Joseph?

03 / *John Carter,
Director of Operations*

SHEPHERDS

"**A**nd in the same region there were shepherds out in the field, keeping watch over their flock by night. And an angel of the Lord appeared to them, and the glory of the Lord shone around them, and they were filled with great fear. And the angel said to them, 'Fear not, for behold, I bring you good news of great joy that will be for all the people.'" Luke 2:8-10

Before we get into the study, take a minute and think about what a shepherd does. In our modern-day society being a shepherd might not signify anything at all, in fact, it would be pretty hard even to describe what a shepherd does. I have never met a shepherd, so to try to describe what they go through would be hard. I would be surprised if someone came up to me and said their occupation was a shepherd, would you? I imagine you would too.

What is the first thing you think of when you think of the occupation of shepherding? _____
_____ *herding animals* _____
_____

Luke chapter 2 points out three things that are involved with shepherding.
    1) It involves being out in the open (field).
    2) It requires extreme vigilance (keeping watch).
    3) It is even done at night.

I am sure there are many other aspects of shepherding, but just off of those three things I would not put it on my top ten list of jobs on my bucket list. Being out in the open, was probably a tactical move so they could see threats coming towards them. Those threats could be anything ranging from bandits to beast. Who in their right mind would sign up to protect sheep and potentially risk their life for them (bandits and beasts would not hesitate to kill a shepherd)? There was no time to slack on the job; any job that requires constant attentive care for any long period is difficult. I imagine a mother (or teacher) that has young children can relate to this. It is a mental challenge of the highest level. I guess shepherding sheep would require the same mental problem. Then to top it off you have to do it in the dark. As if the job was not hard enough with points one and two, they are even on duty at night.

What is one of the scariest things you can imagine a shepherd having to deal with on the job? _____
_____ *being attacked* _____
_____

What is the toughest job you have ever had? _____
_____ *raising children* _____
_____

The purpose of understanding what the shepherds go through is to establish that the men that took on the job of shepherding were not weak, easy to scare people. 1 Samuel 17:34-35 gives David's experience, **"But David said to Saul, 'Your servant used to keep sheep for his father. And when there came a lion, or a bear, and took a lamb from the flock, I went after him and struck him and delivered it out of his mouth. And if he arose against me, I caught him by his beard and struck him and killed him.'"** David as a young man was a shepherd taking on a lion and a bear; he then volunteers to take on a giant. I do not think fear was in his vocabulary. When we read in Luke chapter 2 that the shepherds were **"filled with great fear,"** I believe that it is important to truly comprehend what that meant for these men.

Shepherds

What scares you (I mean really scares you)? _____
_____*failure*_____
_____

What scares us will most definitely look different for each person. You might think of things like:
- Losing my family
- Public speaking
- Death
- Failing people
- The Dark
- Being alone
- Insects

It is likely there are many more things that individuals can list, but consider what filled the shepherds with fear (the glory of the Lord that shone around them). Does that seem like an odd thing for which to be fearful? Have you ever been afraid of God? Have you ever considered His Glory as something to fear? _____
_____*hesitant but don't think fearful*_____
_____

> Exodus 33:16-23
>
> "'For how shall it be known that I have found favor in your sight, I and your people? Is it not in your going with us, so that we are distinct, I and your people, from every other people on the face of the earth?' And the Lord said to Moses, 'This very thing that you have spoken I will do, for you have found favor in my sight, and I know you by name.' Moses said, 'Please show me your glory.' And he said, 'I will make all my goodness pass before you and will proclaim before you my name 'The Lord.' And I will be gracious to whom I will be gracious, and will show mercy on whom I will show mercy. But,' he said,

> *'you cannot see my face, for man shall not see me and live.' And the Lord said, 'Behold, there is a place by me where you shall stand on the rock, and while my glory passes by I will put you in a cleft of the rock, and I will cover you with my hand until I have passed by. Then I will take away my hand, and you shall see my back, but my face shall not be seen.'"*

There is a lot to discuss in these passages. I love this passage, mainly because it helps me comprehend how AWESOME God is. Not awesome as in "He is a cool dude," but awesome in the sense of grandeur, unfathomable power, huge, magnificent, the person of ultimate authority, and someone worthy of awe. God is AWESOME! My hope is that this passage can give a clearer picture of how the glory of God is a legitimate thing to fear.

Does this passage help you understand the glory of God? Does it help you be in awe? _____

Should the word awesome be used for anything (dessert, sporting event, concert) other than God? _No_

> Read Exodus 34:5-8
> *"The Lord descended in the cloud and stood with him there, and proclaimed the name of the Lord. The Lord passed before him and proclaimed, 'The Lord, the Lord, a God merciful and gracious, slow to anger, and abounding in steadfast love and faithfulness, keeping steadfast love for thousands, forgiving iniquity and transgression and sin, but who will by no means clear the guilty, visiting the iniquity of the fathers on the*

> *children and the children's children, to the third and the fourth generation.' And Moses quickly bowed his head toward the earth and worshiped."*

This is a description of the character of God, by God. This is both a description that will incite both fear and joy if properly understood. Often we will read verse 6 and are excited about God, but we must not forget the latter part of verse 7. There can be a lengthy discussion on this passage, but I want to focus on one part. Keeping in mind that this is God describing Himself, you see two contrary thoughts in this one portion of Scripture, **"Keeping steadfast love for thousands, forgiving iniquity and transgression and sin, but who will by no means clear the guilty."**

After all this talk of things that scare us, we need to spend some time on the message from the angel, **"Fear not, for I bring you good news of great joy."**

You are probably thinking at this point that this is hard to follow. Am I to fear God even though the angel says not to be afraid? Your inclination might be to say, "I do not get it, so I think I will put the book down now." Please read to the end so that you do not miss this amazing connection that exists between what to fear and what not to fear.

Considering the season, and if you have any knowledge of the Christmas story, you can probably understand quickly that the "Good News" is Jesus Christ. Now, you might be thinking I just gave away the dramatic reveal; I want to keep the angel's message in keeping with who it was said to (the shepherds) and about.

> Isaiah 40:5-11 says, "'*And the glory of the Lord shall be revealed, and all flesh shall see it together, for the mouth of the Lord has spoken.' A voice says, 'Cry!' And I said, 'What shall I cry?' All flesh is grass, and all its beauty is like the flower of the field. The grass withers, the flower fades when the breath of the Lord blows on it; surely the people are grass. The grass withers, the flower fades, but the word of our God will stand forever. Go on up to a high mountain, O Zion, herald of good news; lift up your voice with strength, O Jerusalem, herald of good news; lift it up, fear not; say to the cities of Judah, 'Behold your God!' Behold, the Lord God comes with might, and his arm rules for him; behold, his reward is with him, and his recompense before him. He will tend his flock like a shepherd; he will gather the lambs in his arms; he will carry them in his bosom, and gently lead those that are with young.*"

The last sentence is key. The shepherds in Luke chapter 2 knew what made a good shepherd. They most likely did not need to have the concept of a good shepherd explained to them. They probably knew really well what a bad shepherd was, who knows maybe even one of them would have been considered a bad shepherd. Jesus has used the concept of shepherding all throughout the Bible to help us understand who we are, who He is, and how we are to comprehend who to fear and who not to fear.

> Matthew 9:36
>
> "*Seeing the people, He felt compassion for them, because they were distressed and dispirited like sheep without a shepherd.*"
>
> Hebrews 13:20
>
> "*Now the God of peace, who brought up from the dead the*

> great Shepherd of the sheep through the blood of the eternal covenant, even Jesus our Lord."

John 10:11
> "I am the good shepherd; the good shepherd lays down His life for the sheep."

What about Jesus being a Good Shepherd comforts you? _____
he is watching out for us at all times, to keep away danger

Mathew 25:32-46
> "Before him will be gathered all the nations, and he will separate people one from another as a shepherd separates the sheep from the goats. And he will place the sheep on his right, but the goats on the left. Then the King will say to those on his right, 'Come, you who are blessed by my Father, inherit the kingdom prepared for you from the foundation of the world. For I was hungry and you gave me food, I was thirsty and you gave me drink, I was a stranger and you welcomed me, I was naked and you clothed me, I was sick and you visited me, I was in prison and you came to me.' Then the righteous will answer him, saying, 'Lord, when did we see you hungry and feed you, or thirsty and give you drink? And when did we see you a stranger and welcome you, or naked and clothe you? And when did we see you sick or in prison and visit you?' And the King will answer them, 'Truly, I say to you, as you did it to one of the least of these my brothers, you did it to me.' Then he will say to those on his left, 'Depart from me, you cursed, into the eternal fire prepared for the devil and his angels. For I was hungry and you gave me no food, I was thirsty and you gave me no drink, I was a stranger and you did not welcome me, naked and you did not clothe me, sick and in prison and

Shepherds

> *you did not visit me.' Then they also will answer, saying, 'Lord, when did we see you hungry or thirsty or a stranger or naked or sick or in prison, and did not minister to you?' Then he will answer them, saying, 'Truly, I say to you, as you did not do it to one of the least of these, you did not do it to me.' And these will go away into eternal punishment, but the righteous into eternal life."*

After reading Matthew 25, you cannot help but figure out that in the end there are only two outcomes. One outcome you should fear, and one should give you great joy.

Write out the two opposing thoughts from the above listed verses:

_____

_____

God says He will forgive iniquity, transgression, and sin, but will by no means clear the guilty. What does that mean? How does this happen and how do you know where you are with God? Romans 3:23 ("**_For all have sinned and fall short of the glory of God._**") sums up the standing of all humanity in comparison to the glory of God. All, in my book, means all. It is not some, not a few, not those over there, but all. I do not know about you, but this is something that is legitimately worth some healthy fear.

This is the part you have to do some soul searching. It is not always an easy thing to do, but I hope you consider all that has been discussed in these few pages and take the time to truly evaluate your standing with an AWESOME God. Does it bring fear when you realize how inadequate we are in comparison to His glory? It does me, but I hope you know that God did not stop with the frightful. He laid out a plan that would help us to understand His great love for us. He sent a child, His child. He sent us this child so that we could hear the words, **"Fear not, for behold, I bring you good news of great joy that will be for all the people."**

The message the shepherds heard way back then is still a message that can be heard today!

Take a second and write down three things that give you joy:
1) family
2) animals
3) friends

This time of year, it is easy to lose sight of that concept of joy. With all the hustle, running around, family coming in from out of town, and having to shop, it is hard to have a minute even to think. The whole point of Christmas is to reflect on Jesus, the Child that was sent by God to give us a way to have real joy. I hope today that one of the things you listed as giving you joy was that you know who God is and you know His Son, Jesus.

humbling

healthy people

Shepherds / Devotion 1

WHY SHEPHERDS?

Isaiah Combs / *Worship Leader and Young Adults Director*

I had a lot of interesting conversations with a lot of very interesting people in my nine years in the military. While I was stationed in Turkey, I began to spend some time with a guy named Aaron Skoog. He was from the mountains of Montana and grew up on a sheep farm. He was a modern day shepherd. I had never met a shepherd. Growing up and learning about the Bible in different gatherings, I had heard the term shepherd many times:

- Joseph's family were shepherds (Genesis 46:34).
- Moses was a shepherd when God called him to free his people (Exodus 3:1).
- David was a shepherd when he was anointed the next king of Israel (1 Samuel 16).
- The prophet Isaiah calls us sheep (Isaiah 53:6).
- The prophet Ezekiel talks about shepherds (Ezekiel 34)
- Shepherds where present at Jesus' birth (Luke 2).
- Jesus told a story of the shepherd (John 10).
- Jesus even calls Himself the Good Shepherd (John 10:11).

I think it is safe to say that shepherding is a common theme in the Bible and that it was put there on purpose for a purpose. Skoog would tell me very funny stories of sheep being extremely dumb. He had to ensure all cliffs were fenced because if one sheep walked off the cliff the rest of his flock would walk off the cliff. They would do the same with water and drown. They were scared all the time and had no way to defend themselves. During birthing season, he would have to sleep in the barn and wake up every two hours so he could help them give birth. If not, the sheep and the lamb would both die.

I feel like I went through shepherding 101. I know the basics, and I will wisely choose never to be involved with sheep. So I also think is it is safe to say that sheep are very, very, very dumb and this is also a common theme in the Bible.

So why are shepherds in the Bible so much? I believe there are three reasons:

1. Shepherds were considered the lowest of the low. Genesis 46:34 says that the Egyptians thought shepherds were the lowest of the low. So why did God choose to use so many shepherds like Joseph, Moses, David, and the shepherds at Jesus birth? John 3:30 says, **"He must increase and I must decrease."** Mathew 11:11 adds, **"Truly, I say to you, among those born of women there has arisen no one greater than John the Baptist. Yet the one who is least in the kingdom of heaven is greater than he."**

   God does not look at that which we focus. When we make ourselves less, we become more to God. Shepherds were the lowest of low in their society, yet God chose to use shepherds in great ways, and to further their importance they were present at Jesus' birth.

2. I hate to tell you this, but people (you and me) are sheep. We are dumb, we stray, we get lost, and we cause havoc. But God loves us anyway. Isaiah 53:6 says, **"All we like sheep have gone astray; we have turned every one to his own way; and the Lord has laid on him the iniquity of us all."** He even sent His Son Jesus to die for our iniquities. I am thankful for a Good Shepherd. John 10:14-15 says, **"I am the good shepherd. I know my own and my own know me, just as the Father knows me and I know the Father; and I lay down my life for the sheep."**

3. He used shepherds that had a lot of practice leading people because we are sheep and need direction.

Shepherds / Devotion 2

GREAT FEAR

Wes McCullough / *Production Director*

Have you ever been outside during a thunderstorm when a giant lightning bolt is followed by a massive boom? In an instant, your legs can go limp and your heart races. A close encounter of a strong thunderstorm makes you feel vulnerable and insignificant. It is not just about the possible physical harm, at that moment you have a renewed respect for the strength of the storm.

> *"And an angel of the Lord appeared to them, and the glory of the Lord shone around them, and they were filled with great fear. And the angel said to them, 'Fear not, for behold, I bring you good news of great joy that will be for all the people.'"*
> Luke 2:9-10

I imagine the surprise of an angel appearing before you is much more intense than a thunder boom. You would probably fall to your knees in their heavenly presence. I do not think you would fear harm from them, but you would certainly have absolute respect for their authority. I believe this is the fear the shepherds experienced in Luke 2 when they were visited by an angel.

The Bible speaks a lot about the fear of the Lord. In many instances, it is in the context of teaching life lessons and promises wisdom, knowledge, and life.

> *"The fear of the Lord leads to life, and whoever has it rests satisfied; he will not be visited by harm."* Proverbs 19:23
>
> *"The fear of the Lord is the beginning of knowledge; fools despise wisdom and instruction."* Proverbs 1:7

> *"The fear of the Lord is the beginning of wisdom, and the knowledge of the Holy One is insight."* Proverbs 9:10
>
> *"For great is the Lord, and greatly to be praised, and he is to be feared above all gods."* 1 Chronicles 16:25
>
> *"For great is the Lord, and greatly to be praised; he is to be feared above all gods."* Psalm 96:4
>
> *"Blessed is the man who fears the Lord, who greatly delights in his commandments!"* Psalm 112:1

If you are always cognizant of God's infinite power and authority, you need not be afraid of the Heavenly Father. Respect His power, His justice, His authority, and always know that He has a plan with your best interests in mind.

Shepherds / Devotion 3

ALL PEOPLE

Richie Henson / *Production Director*

As members of the modern western culture, many of us are ignorant to the social structures prevalent at the time of Jesus' birth. However, if we take just a moment to educate ourselves, the Bible can come alive in a new and special way. This is especially true of the Shepherds in Luke 2.

Shepherds were reviled as lowly and unworthy people. They were shunned from society and forced to stay on the outskirts tending their sheep in the desert. To give some context, the only other group of people reviled as greatly as shepherds were tax collectors. This culture of hatred was perpetrated by the same people who should have included these people, the religious leaders. Suffice it to say, people agreed that shepherds were the worst.

Although it would seem obvious to say that no visit from an angel is ordinary, the cultural context proves this visit to be especially extraordinary. The messenger of God came to a group of men that were on the bottom rung of the societal ladder, and the angel provides such an important message: **"For unto you is born this day in the city of David a Savior, who is Christ the Lord. And this will be a sign for you: you will find a baby wrapped in swaddling cloths and lying in a manger"** (verses 11-12).

What a powerful statement from the angel. He specifically states that Jesus was born for the shepherds. The angel is saying, "Unto you men, out here in the desert living ostracized from society, the Savior is here for you." What a powerful moment in the lives of men who lived a grim reality. In truth, this revelation to the lowest of society concerning the birth of the Messiah makes a huge statement regarding the intention of Jesus' ministry. That is to say, Jesus came for all people.

Often we can be so consumed by position, but as is evidenced by this account, the Gospel is no respecter of position or persons. Jesus came for each one of us whether we live in a mansion on a hill or a box on the side of the road. The message of the angel is clear, Jesus is here to save everyone, and that includes the broken, the abandoned, and the overlooked. May we have the mindset of inclusion this Christmas as we seek to provide the hope of the Gospel to everyone we have the opportunity to meet.

Shepherds / Devotion 4

SINGING IN THE REIGN

Josh Lahring / *Production Director*

Every year when the Christmas season arrives, Christmas music takes over the radio and stores, carolers sing on the streets, and people are in the giving spirit sending gifts to family and friends. The season is filled with joyfulness and giving. It is easy to be joyful when things are going well and you have a lot for which to be thankful. If you had nothing though, could you still be joyful?

One of my favorite songs to sing during the Christmas season is "My soul Magnifies the Lord." It says, "My soul magnifies the Lord, He has done great things for me." We have seen God do some amazing things and we praise His name for that. No matter what we are going through we can be encouraged that God has done great things in our lives. God sending Jesus to this earth and giving Him up as a sacrifice for our sins is the greatest thing He has ever done or ever could do. Even if He never did another thing for us, that is enough to praise Him for the rest of our lives.

This is why we come together as the church and sing. Each of us has seen God do different things in our lives, but there is one common thing that all of us can celebrate and praise God together for, and that is Jesus. No matter if you are at your highest of highs or lowest of lows, you can sing because you know that Jesus is Lord and He came to rescue us. While we praise God together as the church, it is encouraging to think that what we are doing is what a multitude of heavenly hosts did, and are doing, as well (Luke 2:13-14):

"And suddenly there was with the angel a multitude of the heavenly host praising God and saying, 'Glory to God in the highest, and on earth peace among those with whom he is pleased!'"

Shepherds / Devotion 5

HIDE THEN GO SEEK

John Hubbard / *Worship Leader*

I will always remember the first time my family went to Disney World. I was the oldest of four kids so we did not go until I was fourteen. You might think that at fourteen I would be too old to think Disney World would be cool, but even then, as we approached in the car I was training my eyes on the horizon. Nearby was this place I had known of and knew so much about but had never seen and I was so excited to confirm it with my own eyes. I did not doubt that it was real, but there is a certainty that visual confirmation brings, an understanding that I desired to have. I imagine this is only an inkling of the emotions that ran through the shepherds just outside of Bethlehem. In Luke 2:15-16 the shepherds have just witnessed a choir of angels proclaiming the birth of Jesus.

> *"When the angels went away from them into heaven, the shepherds said to one another, 'Let us go over to Bethlehem and see this thing that has happened, which the Lord has made known to us.' And they went with haste and found Mary and Joseph, and the baby lying in a manger."*

The shepherds were on such a roller coaster of emotions in such a short span of time. An angel appeared to them and they were frightened, then many more appeared and began to sing, then just as suddenly as they appeared they were gone. God wanted the shepherds to be a part of something that would be talked about for generations, literally thousands of years. Like most things that will have an eternal significance, the first reaction is fear. Your fear can paralyze you into missing out on God's plan. What if Moses had run from the burning bush? What if he was too afraid to run until afterward (similar to Jonah) once he thought God was not looking? Of course, He was looking all along.

These shepherds overcame their fear of the angels and were filled with excitement at the news they heard. They had an experience of intimate worship with God. Then the shepherds gathered their belongings and went to share a meal. They probably talked about how great they felt, cherishing that awesome chorus when the angels sang or how cool it was when the drums and light show really picked up on the bridge. They could hear the voices so well. Do not forget the sharing of the Word that was so touching and moving. That started to sound a lot like Sunday afternoon lunch, did it not? No, these men did not need to sit and reflect on what had happened. They were going to make sure that they did not miss out on the next thing God was doing. They were so excited about the Good News the angels had brought that they went with haste and found where Jesus had been born, and they worshiped Him there.

Now, reflection and remembering a special moment is a not bad thing, those precious times with God are a foundation of your personal testimony. I know that for me, when God calls and makes it clear when His train is leaving the station, I do not want to miss it because it scares me at first.

Shepherds / Devotion 6

SWEET TWEET

Danielle Hardenburg / *Nursery and Pre-K Director*

"And when they saw it, they made known the saying that had been told them concerning this child. And all who heard it wondered at what the shepherds told them." Luke 2:17-18

The shepherds in the field that night were out doing their jobs. Just another humble day in the life of herding, protecting, and caring for their flock. Just a typical work day, until an angel appeared! This angel told them our Savior was born for all and exactly how they could go and find Him. The shepherds left their flocks and hustled to Bethlehem to see things exactly the way they were told. Our Savior was not in a palace, but in a stable. He was a baby not a man, lying in a manger not resting on a throne. He was not in array, but wrapped in cloth. The angel told the shepherds this infant was the Christ, and they found Him precisely the way they were told they would! They found Him, and spread the word about what they were told and the truth in what they had seen.

When I first came on staff at The River Church, I was asked to write my testimony. My first thought was A: I can barely turn on this Mac, let alone pull my story together on paper, B: I hope someone is an amazing proof reader/spell checker, and C: Why have I not done this already? My family and I have experienced God in some amazing ways and for a long time I was praying to recognize the opportunities to share. However, I surely never thought of writing especially for others to actually read. Yikes! But our testimony starts with knowing our story and being able to tell it. Our story starts with how we first found Jesus. We have been blessed to meet many people who have bravely shared awesome, raw, beautiful stories of where they found our Savior. These testimonies make known our King!

We are living in a time where we can share things instantly. We can share our feelings, activities, ideas, highs or lows in a text, post, blog, or a video whenever the mood strikes us. We can share something simple about our day or something burdensome. We click and can send out anything for the world to hear. Do you take the time to share anything about Christ? Have you shared how you met Him?

04 / *Ryan Story,
Student Pastor*

THE FEAR OF THE LORD IS THE BEGINNING OF KNOWLEDGE

During the Christmas season what words come to mind? Most people would say happy, joyful, jolly, peaceful, wonderful, snowy, merry, or maybe even festive. If you asked a child, they would most likely say no school, presents, family, Santa, or lights. You would not typically see the word 'fear.' When I was a child, I never would have associated Christmas with fear. Oddly enough, *National Geographic* brought a new piece of information to my brain. In European countries, there is folklore that Santa had himself an evil counterpart. While the legend of St. Nicholas was used for motivating children into being nice, Krampus was used to strike fear into children if they were naughty. I remember being told that if I were naughty, Santa would leave me coal. That never seemed to be much of a threat; however, if my parents would have said if I were naughty I would have gotten kidnapped, I think I would have associated Christmas with fear.

How can fear motivate you in a positive way? _____
I can do all things through christ who strengthens me

Why can fear motivate you in a negative way? _____

Fear is an interesting word in the Bible. When we first hear or read the word fear, we sometimes associate that word more with Halloween rather than Christmas. We associate fear more with the devil than we do Jesus. The last few weeks we have studied Mary, Joseph, and the shepherds, and how they were frightful when they gazed upon angels and heavenly hosts. So was God sending angels to frighten people? That does not sound like an all-loving God. We can create massive misconceptions if we use *Webster's Dictionary* to figure out word meaning.

Fear of the Lord

When we look up 'fear' in a Bible dictionary or a *Strong's Concordance* you might see something like this:

yir'ah- *fear, terror, fearing*
A. *fear, terror*
B. *awesome or terrifying thing (object causing fear)*
C. *fear (of God), respect, reverence, piety*
D. *revered*

In most cases in the Bible when we see the word 'fear' we have to go with a mixture of all those meanings. When the shepherds saw the heavenly hosts they were probably full of terror, a numerous amount of angels became visible! They were also full of fear of reverence because they were visited by heavenly beings. So when Mary saw the angel, I am sure she was spooked out of her mind, but based on her response to the angel, she also had a healthy dose of respect and reverence.

When you hear the term 'fear the Lord' what comes to your mind?
respect, honor
— not scared —

Why can this term be misleading to the un-churched? _____

Let us now put together one of the most powerful verses in the Bible.

> Proverbs 9:10
> *"The fear of the Lord is the beginning of wisdom, and the knowledge of the Holy One is insight."*

84

If we use our newly found exegetical information, we can figure out how to unlock the awesomeness of this verse.

Which definition would you say fits best with Proverbs 9? _____
_____C_____

While each definition of fear could work here, I lean towards C.

Now, if we reword the verse:
"*Reverent respect of the Lord is the beginning of wisdom.*"

This gives a more accurate conclusion.

How does respect for God bring the beginning of wisdom? _____
_____*Wise choices*_____

What is wisdom? Why is it important? _____
_____

Read James 1:5

How do we get wisdom? _____
_____

When most people start thinking of the Christmas story, respect and wisdom are not the first things that pop into their mind. But if we take the Proverb's verse and look at Mary, Joseph, or the shepherd's life we can see that they had this verse stored in their heart. Mary and Joseph listened to the angel with respect and honor, which brought about them being wise by accepting God's plan for their lives. When the angels showed themselves to the shepherds, they respected them at their word and went to Bethlehem to find Jesus. Proper respect can bring about wise life choices.

This Christmas, how can proper reverence for Jesus bring about a wise choice? _____
_____
_____

Fear of the Lord / Devotion 1

A U T O P H O B I A

Max Sinclair / *Children's Director*

Autophobia is the fear of abandonment. Being alone is scary. I remember being a kid in a grocery store with my parents and something caught my eye. I stopped and looked and wondered about all this toy was, but I lost my parents. They kept walking and I could not remember where they were. Instantly, I became stressed, I was alone and I was afraid. My story is not just a story that is a parents and a child's nightmare, but us being alone is a real and present fear. Our story of being left alone is sometimes what we feel like when we go through life and cannot feel the presence of God.

Throughout our lives, we need to remember that our God is with us through His Holy Spirit. Even at the beginning of the church, at the day of Pentecost, we were given the Great Comforter, the Holy Spirit. With this being said, that raises the question of why do we sometimes feel abandoned and alone? The answer is we are running from His presence and are not listening to His voice. The fact remains He is there to be loved and to show you love like a Father to His child. In Hebrews 13:5 we are reminded of the promise of God "**...I will never leave you nor forsake you.**"

That is our God; He is not a God who will let us be alone. He even said at creation that it is not good for man to be alone. We need and crave a relationship with God. Like a child lost in the supermarket, we need to remember that our God is not gone, He is just where we He needs to be. As a Christian and a child of God we have been given eternal life: "**And this is the testimony, that God gave us eternal life, and this life is in his Son. Whoever has the Son has life; whoever does not have the Son of God does not have**

life. I write these things to you who believe in the name of the Son of God, that you may know that you have eternal life" (1 John 5:11-13).

Through Christ we are given eternal life. It is an eternal life to spend with Him and He with us.

Fear of the Lord / Devotion 2

MONOPHOBIA

Max Sinclair / *Children's Director*

Monophobia is the fear of being alone. Many times in my time in the service I felt alone. I can recall clearly the time I was in boot camp, we had just finished everything and we were prepping for bed, I grabbed my Bible and sat near my rack. I opened the Bible to the Gospel of John and I began to read. As I read, others around began to ask questions and began to look down on me for what I was doing. One of the guys in my division came up and began to tell me how my faith was worthless. He scowled how my God was weak, how He had not saved me. He even said how no matter what I read it was a bunch of made up tales meant to control the masses. At that moment, being a church kid, I never felt more alone. I never felt more scared, vulnerable, and persecuted. My life was built on the faith that what Jesus had done, He had done for not just me but all of humanity. He died for all of our sins, for us to have a relationship with Him. Tears streaming down my eyes, I laid in my rack hiding my face as to not be seen by others. The fear of being alone is such a crippling fear. We are not meant to be alone, and that fear, that doubt, will crush and break an individual as it almost did to me.

In Acts we see the history of the church in all of its splendor. An account by the physician Luke takes a look at the apostle Paul who was being tried before the ruling council in Jerusalem. In Acts 22, the story unfurls in a beautiful way. Paul is brought before the council and testifies that he believes in the redeeming power of Jesus and how He changes lives as He changed Paul's own life. As he tells his testimony to the ruling council, the Pharisees and the Sadducees began to argue about what he says. In the midst of the argument the Lord was standing with Paul and said to him ***"Take courage,***

for as you have testified to the facts about me in Jerusalem, so you must testify also in Rome" (Acts 23:11). In the midst of a trying time, the Lord will be with you as He was with Paul in the most trying time.

Fear of the Lord / Devotion 3

GAMOPHOBIA

Dr. Randy T. Johnson / *Growth Pastor*

Gamophobia comes from the Greek word 'Gamos' which means marriage and 'Phobos' meaning fear. It can be the fear of marriage, but it is defined larger than that; it is the fear of commitment.

Psalm 37:5 says, **"Commit your way to the Lord; trust in him, and he will act."** Following the Lord is the key to success. The verse even says, "He will act." When we choose to follow the Lord, He will get involved. He will show up. David uses several other directives in writing this chapter: **"Trust in the Lord"** (verse 3), **"Delight yourself in the Lord"** (verse 4), and **"Be still before the Lord"** (verse 7). Commitment is essential and involves focus with a willingness to act.

Pilate was not willing to commit to the Lord. He knew Jesus was innocent, but folded. Matthew 27:24 says, **"So when Pilate saw that he was gaining nothing, but rather that a riot was beginning, he took water and washed his hands before the crowd, saying, 'I am innocent of this man's blood; see to it yourselves."** It is sad. Pilate was self-reflecting and **'saw that he was gaining nothing.'** Pilate was committed to himself. It did not end well for him. He had an excellent opportunity to step up and take a stand for the Lord. He cowered. He probably did not want to lose his position, financial status, and 'upright' reputation.

Charles Stanley has said, "Too many Christians have a commitment of convenience. They'll stay faithful as long as it's safe and doesn't involve risk, rejection, or criticism. Instead of standing alone in the face of challenge or temptation, they check to see which way their friends are going." We need to be willing to step outside of our comfort zone and make a difference in the life of people we know and those we do not know yet. The legendary football coach, Vince Lombardi, made a statement about his football team that relates to the church, "Individual commitment to a group effort — that is what makes a team work, a company work, a society work, a civilization work." Together we are better. We need to commitment to the Lord, His work, and His people.

"It was character that got us out of bed, commitment that moved us into action, and discipline that enabled us to follow through." Zig Ziglar

Fear of the Lord / Devotion 4

PANOPHOBIA

Dr. Randy T. Johnson / *Growth Pastor*

Panophobia or Pantophobia comes from the Greek word 'Pan' or 'Panto' meaning 'all' and 'Phobos' meaning fear. It is the fear of all or everything. The word 'panic' is derived from the name of the Greek god 'Pan.' This is the fear that is associated with panic or anxiety. It is the fear that something bad is going to happen.

You have probably heard this quote before even though we do not know who said it, "I do not know what the future holds, but I know who holds the future." Take a moment and think through that phrase. Tomorrow might catch us off guard, but it will not catch God by surprise. Romans 8:28 says, **"And we know that for those who love God all things work together for good, for those who are called according to his purpose."** We do not know what tomorrow may bring, but God is there. He is in control. He has a plan. He is watching out for us. Going further into Romans 8 we read, **"What then shall we say to these things? If God is for us, who can be against us? He who did not spare his own Son but gave him up for us all, how will he not also with him graciously give us all things?"** God held His Word in providing salvation for us. He will provide for us in the future. Abraham had to experience anxiety in offering up his son Isaac, but God showed up. Abraham felt so blessed that he named the place **"The Lord will provide"** (Genesis 22:14).

The key is to 'let go, and let God.' It is the mindset that we give the controls of our life to the Lord. We stop pushing our personal agendas and seek His plans. Proverbs 3:5-6 say, **"Trust in the Lord with all your heart, and do not lean on your own understanding.**

In all your ways acknowledge him, and he will make straight your paths. " Trust God with today and tomorrow. Give Him full access to your resources and your calendar. He will make them better.

> *"For I know the plans I have for you, declares the Lord, plans for welfare and not for evil, to give you a future and a hope."*
> *Jeremiah 29:11*

Fear of the Lord / Devotion 5

N O M O P H O B I A

Noble Baird / *Community Center Director*

In 1983, the world was introduced to the first commercially available cell phone. The DynaTAC 8000 hit retail shelves in 1984 at the low price of $3,995! Amazingly, this phone had a battery life to last for 30 minutes of talk time and only took 10 hours to charge. Fast forward over three decades and over 95% of Americans own a cellphone, with 75% being smartphones. As our culture here in America continues to grow, become more fast-paced, and our schedules continue to fill, we have become dependent on these little devices in our pockets.

For many of us, it is through these busy schedules that we are able to provide for our families and able to give back to God a portion of the blessing He has given us. However, in this fast-paced culture, we can often forget to take a step back and breath. In Psalm 46:10, David writes (as God is speaking through him), **"Be still and know that I am God. I will be exalted among the nations, I will be exalted in the earth!"** Jesus understood what it meant to be still. Yes, He had a busy schedule during His ministry here on earth. He was constantly traveling, speaking, healing, and He had twelve men He was discipling the whole way! However, countless times throughout the New Testament, we read of how Jesus took time to rest, pray, and remember His Father who was in control of it all.

Nomophobia, is the fear of being out of cell signal range or without our cellphones. If I am completely honest, there have been times in my life where this fear was very real in my life. However, when I remember the words of David and the actions of Christ, that fear is taken away. Now, I am not saying that cellphones are evil and we should not have them. Being in ministry, my phone has given me the ability to pray with people who are hundreds of miles away, video chat my missionary friends overseas, and has helped me get to Canada and back without a big outdated map! Yet, this reminder to be still, is crucial in the business of the world we live in. So, as you continue your week, I challenge you to take some time to set your phone down and truly just disconnect. Take some time to pray, rest, and remember the One who is in control. Be still.

Fear of the Lord / Devotion 6

THANATOPHOBIA

Noble Baird / *Community Center Director*

Thanatophobia. If I was a betting man, I would bet that this is a fear with which a majority of the world struggles. This fear, is the fear of death. At the time of writing this devotional, noon, it is estimated that there have already been a total of almost 80,000 deaths in the world today. We have all experienced the affects of death in some capacity. Whether it be the loss of a family member, friend, co-worker, teacher, or maybe a favorite public figure, we have all suffered because of death. However, thanatophobia is a fear that can be overcome.

In Genesis 3, we have what is often referred to as "The Fall." This was the time in our history, when Adam and Eve were overcome by temptation and sinned against God. From that moment, sin entered the perfect world which God created. As a penalty for this sin, death also entered into our world. As God's Word and our history has unfolded over the course of thousands of years, life and death have been a constant. As new life enters our world, life also leaves it. Fast forward to the night where angels rejoiced and shepherds traveled to worship a King; God gave us a Savior who would pay the penalty for a fear which has plagued this world since it became corrupt. As we read through the Gospels, we see our Savior Jesus conquering over death. He came with a purpose and a plan, which was fulfilled at the cross and in the tomb that was emptied three days later.

Death is very real and if I am honest with all of you, it has been a fear that I struggled with at a time in my life. Yet, when I take a step back and remember the Savior who conquered death for me, before I was even born, I am reminded of Paul's words in 1 Corinthians 15:55, **"O death, where is your victory? O death, where is your sting?"**

As I finish writing today, the death count has now risen to an estimated 82,000. Yes, death is very real and yes it is scary. However, as followers of Christ, death should not give us a fear, but a sense of urgency. An urgency to proclaim the Gospel and to make sure that we do everything within our power to share the message and love of our amazing Savior who conquered the fear that plagues so many in our world today. So, when you have those times of fear, take a step back and proclaim those words boldly as Paul did, for we have already won the war and we will spend eternity with our Savior! **"O death, where is your victory? O death, where is your sting?"**

**05 / Pastor Jayson Combs,
Family Pastor**

HEROD

Herod

One of the scariest moments of my life occurred when I completely lost control of my car. I was driving 75 miles per hour down the highway when my car hydroplaned in the heavy rain and I began to spin out of control. I did three circles in the middle of the highway. It was a little bit like slow motion as I spun around. First I saw the guard rail, then the trees, then the guard rail, and the trees again. Finally, I stopped spinning and found myself looking perfectly straight ahead in my lane. A quick sigh of relief and I continued driving down the highway with a tighter grip and palpitating heart.

Have you ever lost control of something? (Examples…car, lawn mower, hair clippers, temper, skis, etc.) _____
_____
_____

Where was your fear level at the time? (Let's just say, I drove a little slower the rest of the way home!) _____
_____
_____

> Matthew 2:1-12, 16
> *"Now after Jesus was born in Bethlehem of Judea in the days of Herod the king, behold, wise men from the east came to Jerusalem, saying, 'Where is he who has been born king of the Jews? For we saw his star when it rose and have come to worship him.' When Herod the king heard this, he was troubled, and all Jerusalem with him; and assembling all the chief priests and scribes of the people, he inquired of them where the Christ was to be born. They told him, 'In Bethlehem of Judea, for so it is written by the prophet: 'And you, O Bethlehem, in the land of Judah, are by no means least among the rulers of Judah; for from you shall come a ruler who will*

> shepherd my people Israel." Then Herod summoned the wise men secretly and ascertained from them what time the star had appeared. And he sent them to Bethlehem, saying, 'Go and search diligently for the child, and when you have found him, bring me word, that I too may come and worship him.' After listening to the king, they went on their way. And behold, the star that they had seen when it rose went before them until it came to rest over the place where the child was. When they saw the star, they rejoiced exceedingly with great joy. And going into the house, they saw the child with Mary his mother, and they fell down and worshiped him. Then, opening their treasures, they offered him gifts, gold and frankincense and myrrh. And being warned in a dream not to return to Herod, they departed to their own country by another way."
>
> "Then Herod, when he saw that he had been tricked by the wise men, became furious, and he sent and killed all the male children in Bethlehem and in all that region who were two years old or under, according to the time that he had ascertained from the wise men."

Why do you think the birth of Jesus would trouble Herod and the people in Jerusalem? *no competition*

Why do you think he would meet with the chief priests and scribes?

What did Herod tell the wise men he 'wanted' to do? _____
_____
_____

History tells us that Herod was a king who would do whatever it took to keep his power and control. It is said he had his wife and multiple sons killed because they posed a threat to his reign. Scripture also tells us that he had all the male babies under two years of age killed in Bethlehem because he did not want the potential King of the Jews to survive. Herod did anything and everything he could to keep things under his control.

What do you suppose would drive someone to be that out of control?
_____
_____
_____

> James 3:13-16
> *"Who is wise and understanding among you? By his good conduct let him show his works in the meekness of wisdom. But if you have bitter jealousy and selfish ambition in your hearts, do not boast and be false to the truth. This is not the wisdom that comes down from above, but is earthly, unspiritual, demonic. For where jealousy and selfish ambition exist, there will be disorder and every vile practice."*

According to the book of James, what is the result of jealousy and selfish ambition? _____
_____
_____

Bitter jealousy and selfish ambition controlled every decision and action in Herod's life. What decisions and actions in your life have been easily controlled by something other than God? _____

_____

_____

Herod was afraid that Jesus was coming to take control. What areas of your life do you struggle to give over to God's control? How can the words of 2 Corinthians 5:14 (**"For the love of Christ controls us, because we have concluded this: that one has died for all, therefore all have died."**) encourage us and give us hope? _____

_____

I have read a lot about Lee Strobel and am excited a movie is coming out on his spiritual journey. Strobel was the former legal editor of the Chicago Tribune. He graduated from an Ivy League School and was a stout atheist. He thought the idea of a loving creator was a 'stupid' idea. His wife came home one day and told him that she had decided to follow Jesus Christ. Of course, this was devastating news to Lee, and he believed his marriage would crumble. He believed that if his wife was controlled by religion, he wanted nothing to do with it.

Over the next few months, his wife's actions were surprisingly attractive to him. Lee finally attended a church service with her, but with hidden intentions to help pull her out the religious cult. That day, however, he heard the real story of Jesus Christ. For the next year and a half, Lee researched the story of Jesus for himself. In the end, he confessed Jesus to be his Lord and Savior and wrote an influential and best-selling book, "*The Case for Christ.*"

Thinking about Lee's story, it is amazing to realize the real impact of Lee's wife. She was a lady who put her life under God's control and watched God do amazing things through her life. She followed His lead into the major life changing events.

Herod

Jesus came to this earth many years ago not only to die on the cross but to become the King of our lives. He is to be the central controlling factor in all that we do.

What is the biggest thing that holds you back from giving Jesus the keys to your life? _____
_____
_____

Herod / Devotion 1

WISE MEN WITH BAD NEWS

Mark O'Connor / *Student Director*

Imagine with me if you will for a moment. You are sitting at work one day, three guys you have never seen before walk up and ask for the new guy. I do not know what it is you do, but when you ask them who exactly they are looking for, they say it is the guy who is replacing you. How do you feel at that point? You are just going about your day when you find out you are done in your current position. Most of us would be a bit panicked, probably very uneasy. I would venture to say there would be a bit of anger there as well. This is what happened to a guy named Herod. He is sitting on his throne when this happens in Matthew 2:1-2,

> *"Now after Jesus was born in Bethlehem of Judea in the days of Herod the king, behold, wise men from the east came to Jerusalem, saying, 'Where is he who has been born king of the Jews? For we saw his star when it rose and have come to worship him.'"*

It was pretty shocking news for Herod. I am sure it was the same feeling we get when there is some unexpected bad news. I feel like I have been punched in the gut and a weight comes over me that can sometimes cause me to react in quite an unreasonable manner. Thankfully that does not happen very much and I am much better equipped to handle it these days. But Herod did not, and we will examine later through this week how well he did not handle this terrible news.

But was it really that bad? Maybe for him. Certainly, not for us. In fact, Luke lays it out quite clearly in chapter 2 when a group of shepherds find out from an angel that Jesus had been born:

> *"And the angel said to them, 'Fear not, for behold, I bring you good news of great joy that will be for all the people. For unto you is born this day in the city of David a Savior, who is Christ the Lord. And this will be a sign for you: you will find a baby wrapped in swaddling cloths and lying in a manger.'"*

A Savior is born. Yep, pretty great news for us. We celebrate this incredible event every year and rightly so. We often forget about this dark time that came as result of such a miraculous event. Some people have never even heard of this king named Herod. Take in the whole story and grow in your relationship with God and in your knowledge of His Word this Christmas season.

Herod / Devotion 2

MY KINGDOM

Brett Eberle / *Production Director*

Have you ever wondered what it would be like to be king? Do you think about what it would be like to have everything that you ever wanted? Do you dream about what it would be like to know that your kids and their kids would be set up for life? Now, can you imagine what it would be like to have all of this ripped from your hands with nothing you could do to stop it? This is exactly what happened to King Herod when Jesus was born. Most people remember Herod for the terrible thing that he did surrounding the birth of Jesus; they do not remember what he had built, they remember a single choice to commit one of the greatest atrocities in the Bible. But have you ever taken a moment to try and understand why he would have done such a thing? It is helpful to take a minute and explore some of the things that could have driven King Herod to such an extreme.

The first thing that happened was when King Herod's advisors came to him and told him that the baby from the prophecies had been born. Jesus had something that Herod could never have no matter how hard he tried; He had prophecies. There was no mistaking that Jesus was the One, by the end of His time on earth Jesus would fulfill more than three hundred prophecies!

The second thing that helped push Herod to murder was the betrayal from the wise men. Herod gave these wise men an order, an order that if disobeyed would almost certainly mean death, and they disobeyed him. King Herod would have known there was only one reason that he would have been disobeyed, which is whatever the wise men found was more important to them than their lives. This decision would have to confirm all of the suspicions that Herod was having about the legitimacy of the claims that Jesus was alive. He probably wondered, if this infant Jesus could turn the wise men, what would stop Him from turning every Jew once He gets older?

Both of these events add up to the true reason why King Herod committed the terrible atrocity as recorded in the Bible. That reason is the title of this devotion, My Kingdom. Herod saw the series of events that would eventually lead to the downfall of his kingdom. What Herod forgot is something that is very easy and honestly quite common for us to forget as well. He forgot that nothing we have is truly ours. Everything that we have in the world is given to us by God, and the moment that we forget, we are dangerously close to doing what Herod did. When we start to think that anything we have is because we earned it or because we deserve it, we start building our kingdom. As soon as our kingdom starts to appear instead of relying on God to get us through, we rely on ourselves and try to hold onto what we think is ours with everything in our power.

During this time of year, it is easy to get caught up in possessions, but remember no matter what you have or do not have, it is all God's, and nothing that you can do or will do will change that.

Herod / Devotion 3

DRAMA KING

James Clouse / *Student Pastor*

Growing up is hard. Being in student ministry and in and out of schools on a frequent basis, you see some of the struggles that students go through. One of the biggest struggles that students and adults alike experience on a regular basis is drama. Whether this drama is workplace drama or family drama, we have all experienced people in our lives that like to cause it. Herod was one of those people that liked drama.

Herod heard from the wise men that there was a new King of the Jews. This caused a stir with Herod as well as the corrupt religious and government leaders. Matthew 2:3 explains how Herod was feeling, **"When Herod the king heard this, he was troubled, and all Jerusalem with him."**

But Herod could not leave this news alone, he had to cause some drama within the religious leaders. He went on to assemble all the religious leaders and scribes of the time to see what was going on.

This mad man rushed around the city to find out as much as he could about who was threatening his precious kingdom. Verse 6 provides us with a look back to the prophet Micah and I want to focus on a part of this prophecy for a moment, **"And you, O Bethlehem, in the land of Judah, are by no means least among the rulers of Judah; for from you shall come a ruler who will shepherd my people Israel."**

Shepherds are leaders of their flock. They lead the flock in the direction that the shepherd intends. When there is strife, or drama, amongst the flock it is up to the shepherd to lead the flock in the right direction.

In life there will be people who want to cause drama and strife in your life and throw things into chaos. But if we realize that there is one True Shepherd of our lives then we will not let anyone else but our shepherd lead us. The religious leaders of the time let Herod cause un-needed drama that led to Herod trying to kill Jesus. It went so far that he even killed many innocent little boys. Do not let the un-needed drama of the workplace or family drama cause you to stumble in you following Christ.

Herod / Devotion 4

LIAR, LIAR, PANTS ON FIRE

Kyle Wendel / *Children and Student's Director*

Lying is something that we can all say we have done before. Whether it was a small silly lie or a real serious one, we have all lied. Lying can have some real repercussions as well. Lying is never a good thing. We never really benefit from a lie. Eventually the truth will come out or you will burn inside from that lie. As we continue to talk about Herod, we need to look at this next Scripture.

> Matthew 2:7-9 says, *"Then Herod summoned the wise men secretly and ascertained from them what time the star had appeared. And he sent them to Bethlehem, saying, 'Go and search diligently for the child, and when you have found him, bring me word, that I too may come and worship him.' After listening to the king, they went on their way. And behold, the star that they had seen when it rose went before them until it came to rest over the place where the child was."*

Most of us have heard about the wise men that went to see Jesus from the nativity story right? Did you know that King Herod sent some of those men to find Jesus? Herod had heard the story going around that a new king had been born, but he did not want to be overthrown as king or anything like that. So Herod had a secret plan to find this child and destroy him. Herod gathered the wise men and gave them a big fat lie. He told them to go find this child so that he could go and worship this child as well. He wanted the wise men to report back after they found him.

Herod had his pants on fire! But the wise men missed that Herod's pants were on fire as he told them this lie until God revealed the truth to them down the road. Herod really did not want to go worship

Jesus, he wanted to kill Him! We see later in chapter two that Herod went and killed all the male babies in this area. His lie turned into a huge mess. Herod went from wanting one child killed to having every male baby killed. That is a massive transition!

Lies never really have good intentions anyways. Lies do nothing but end up making the situation worse. Lying is the original sin as well. Sin never brings anything good into your life. Sin is what separates us from God. Why would we want to do that?

> Proverbs 12:22 adds, *"Lying lips are an abomination to the Lord, but those who act faithfully are his delight."*

Lying is an abomination to the Lord. We need to remember that lying is never from God. As followers of Christ, we need to constantly pursue the things of God. How do you need to work on lying in your life? It could be small lies you tell or some big ones. Maybe you even lie to yourself. Whatever it is, we need to be people filled with truth. Those who act faithfully are God's delight. We need to want to delight in the Lord. Get rid of those lies in your life, you do not need them. They are not helping.

Herod / Devotion 5

COLLATERAL DAMAGE

Tommy Youngquist / *Children's Pastor*

"Then Herod, when he saw that he had been tricked by the wise men, became furious, and he sent and killed all the male children in Bethlehem and in all that region who were two years old or under, according to the time that he had ascertained form the wise men. Then was fulfilled what was spoken by the prophet Jeremiah: A voice was heard in Ramah, weeping and loud lamentation, Rachel weeping for her children; she refused to be comforted, because they are no more." Matthew 2:16-18

Oh Snap! Here we go with another prophecy in the Old Testament being fulfilled. Imagine the scene. Jesus had just been born. You know, the King of Kings. So naturally the king of those days (Herod) gets a little peanut butter and jealous. Herod wants Jesus dead. So, he sets up a plan to try and make it happen. Herod tries to manipulate the *"We three kings of Orient are, Bearing gifts we traverse afar"* into finding Jesus and telling him where He is. Plan fails! Herod gets super mad that his evil plot did not work so he makes a decree to kill all male babies under two. Do you remember Moses and Pharaoh? What is it with these crazy kings wanting to kill babies? Anyways, an angel of the Lord had told Joseph to go to Egypt before the decree came out so baby Jesus was safe. Phew!

The first question I would like to pose to you is: How would you react if you were a parent of one of those "under two year olds" that was murdered by Herod's decree? What if your child was collateral damage in this scenario? When Jeremiah's prophecy is fulfilled, the Bible tells us how Rachel reacted. She **"wept for her children; she refused to be comforted, because they are no more."**

I am a parent now. The love that I feel for my daughter is unexplainable. I could not imagine being Rachel and losing her children, not child, children. I believe she got very angry and bitter at God for what happened. Look at everything from her point of view. Her children died because of a king that wanted Jesus dead.

The second question I would like to ask you is: Do you blame God for the bad things that happen in your life? God gave us free will. Personally, I am very thankful for the right to choose. Along with free will though, comes consequences for your choices. Good consequences for good decisions and bad consequences for bad decisions. In Genesis, one man made a bad decision and the consequence was this icky thing called sin that was passed to all of humanity. But we need to get real, if it was not Adam it would have been someone else, and for sure me.

I hate sin! I believe it is the reason bad things happen in this world. It is not God's fault for letting us choose. How could we truly love someone that made us love Him. We can choose God or not choose God. What about you? Are you going to blame sin and learn to hate it for the bad things that happen in this world? Are you going to choose God and trust that He is almighty, loving, and faithful? Do you realize He has a plan for you even when bad things happen? God created a way for us to defeat sin when Jesus was born, lived, died, and rose for us. Do not be sin's collateral damage.

Herod / Devotion 6

DEATH OF A MADMAN

Eric Jeffrey

Herod was a brutal man who killed his father-in-law, some of his many wives, and two of his sons. He ignored the laws of God and chose the favor of Rome over his own people. Herod levied huge taxes to pay for his lavish projects which forced an unfair burden on the Jewish citizens he ruled over. He also ordered the deaths of all the male babies in Bethlehem because he perceived the baby Jesus as a threat (Matthew 2:16). To say he was not popular amongst his constituents would probably be an understatement for sure.

The death of Herod is not so well documented in the biblical text; however, Flavius Josephus a Jewish historian, details Herod's death in great detail: As Herod's health began to swiftly deteriorate, he moved to his winter residence in Jericho. Among his ailments recorded by Josephus, "He had a fever, though not a raging fever, an intolerable itching of the whole skin, continuous pains in the intestines, tumors of the feet as in dropsy, inflammation of the abdomen, and gangrene of the privy parts." With a broken and failing body his mind was not far behind. Before his death, Herod devised a plan to execute men from every village from one end of Judea to the other. This was to take place upon the very moment he died. His sick mind reasoned that their death would take away any joy in Judea over his death. The order was never carried out.

Herod was undoubtedly a bitter enemy of the Messiah. Surely one would expect, from a purely human vantage point, that the Jews might enjoy some sense of relief and satisfaction in his death, but no such distinction is made in Matthew's account. It simply has it, **"And when Herod was dead."** The restraint of the biblical writers is contrary to urges of human reasoning that states "he got what he deserved" or maybe "he had that coming" but this may be a testimony to the power of the Gospel.

Osama bin Laden, one of the most notorious men of our time, founder and head of the terror group Al-Qaeda, was fatally shot in Pakistan on May 2, 2011 by United States Navy Seals. Al-Qaeda confirmed the death on May 6 with posts made on militant websites, vowing to avenge the killing. Other Pakistani militant groups, also vowed retaliation against the U.S. and against Pakistan for not preventing the operation. The raid that produced the expiration of Bin Laden was supported by over 90% of the American public, was welcomed by the United Nations, NATO, the European Union, and a large number of governments.

I remember exactly where I was when the report of Bin Laden's death came in. I found myself thinking on one hand, I was relieved that a man responsible for so many deaths was finally brought to justice. On the other hand, I was saddened knowing that someone who by all accounts never confessed Christ had passed from life to death. I questioned within myself the reaction, asking myself which emotion was more appropriate, more Christian? Should I rejoice at bin Laden's death ... or mourn it?

After the announcement was made that the world's most infamous terrorist was indeed dead, Pastor Rick Warren sent out Proverbs 21:15, which says, **"When justice is done, it brings joy to the righteous but terror to evildoers."** It was afterwards reported that Warren's tweet became the third most tweeted verse on this subject. I do not believe that Mr. Warren believes that bin Laden got what he deserved, nor that the passage he quoted means that either. I think the media in all of its wisdom reported it that way.

But, is it the place of the church to rejoice in the death of one clearly an enemy of the faith? Scripture is quite clear on this point. Deuteronomy 32:35 says, **"Vengeance is mine, and recompense, for the time when their foot shall slip; for the day of their calamity is at hand, and their doom comes swiftly."** And later Paul makes reference in Romans, **"Beloved, never avenge yourselves, but leave it to the wrath of God, for it is written, 'Vengeance is mine, I will repay, says the Lord"** (Romans 12:19). The heart of the church should be this: **"Say to them: As I live, says the Lord Jehovah, I have no delight in the death of the wicked, except in the turning of the wicked from his way, and so to live. Turn, turn from your evil ways; for why will you die, O house of Israel?"** (Ezekiel 33:11). By the way, if you are a follower of Christ, you are the church.

When someone dies, friend or enemy, without the knowledge of Christ, it is a victory for the evil one. When a Christian points the finger in the face of the wicked getting what they deserve and shouts for joy, it only reveals that they have forgotten their encounter with grace. How can we celebrate God's saving grace in our own lives on Sunday morning and celebrate retributive justice for others on Sunday evening? Friends pray for enemies and love those that despitefully persecute you!

06 / *Noble Baird,*
Community Center Director

REACH

Last March, I was approached by Pastor Caleb and Pastor Chuck about the possibility of me moving into a new position here at the church. The new position as the Community Center Director would entail me moving into an outreach position here in Holly. In the new position, I would be running our clothing closet and food pantry, along with the goal of reaching into the community loving and helping them in any way possible. Simply put, it is meeting not only the spiritual needs of the community, but the physical needs first.

What are some of the physical needs that our communities face? *poverty, single parenting*

Why is it important to meet the physical needs of a community before their spiritual ones? *help them believe god is good*

The book of James is a hard book for me to read. Often, when I go back and reread passages, it can be a big slap in the face! However, I love the hard hitting truths and James' approach to how we, as followers of Christ, ought to live our lives. In James 2, James writes about being partial in our interactions with others.

What does it mean to be partial? *? unsure*

Have you ever experienced someone being partial against you?
_____
_____
_____

Can you recount a time in your life where you have been susceptible to this? _____
_____
_____

James 2:1-4 says, **"My brothers, show no partiality as you hold the faith in our Lord Jesus Christ, the Lord of glory. For if a man wearing a gold ring and fine clothing comes into your assembly, and a poor man in shabby clothing also comes in, and if you pay attention to the one who wears the fine clothing and say, 'You sit here in a good place,' while you say to the poor man, 'You stand over there,' or, 'Sit down at my feet,' have you not then made distinctions among yourselves and become judges with evil thoughts?"** In this passage, James establishes for us what it means to be partial, and how a simple act of partiality, can quickly escalate to judgment. In the culture we live in, it is easy to fall into this snare of judgment. However, James sets the record and makes it clear about the distinction in God's eyes. In James 2:5 he writes, **"Listen, my beloved brothers, has not God chosen those who are poor in the world to be rich in faith and heirs of the kingdom, which he has promised those who love him?"**

Who has God chosen to be heirs of the kingdom? _____
The poor _____
_____

What has God promised to those who love Him? _____
Kingdom

James takes it a step further and reminds the people of the Law, which was established thousands of years before Christ came and before James was even born! In James 2:8 he says, **"If you really fulfill the royal law according to the Scripture, 'You shall love your neighbor as yourself,' you are doing well."**

What passage of the Old Testament is James referring to here?

Who is your neighbor? _everyone_

Growing up in church, I have always heard this saying which James writes and which Jesus often spoke. It was not until I began my position as Community Center Director that this passage truly came to life. Daily, we get calls from people asking for help in some capacity. Calls range from the shut-ins who have no way to make it out to the center for food, the grandma whose grandkids are getting caught up with the wrong crowd and she is in need of prayer, or the single mom who simply needs help moving some furniture. In all of these things, we as a church are given the opportunity to meet the needs of our neighbors here in our community.

Now, James has just established for us what we ought to do as followers of Christ, what distinction our Heavenly Father sees, and has given us scriptural backing for who we are supposed to love and reach. However, James also gives us the flip side to all of this, for those who still show partiality. In James 2:9-10, James warns us of the outcome for showing partiality, **"But if you show partiality, you are committing sin and are convicted by the law as transgressors. For whoever keeps the whole law but fails in one point has become guilty of all of it."**

What are you convicted by when showing partiality? _____
_____
_____

How much of the Law are we supposed to strive to uphold, as a follower of Christ? _____
_____ *all of it* _____
_____

So, what does this all mean in light of Reach? As a church and as followers of Christ, outreach is an essential part of our walk with Him. If we are all honest, none of us would be here today as followers of Christ, unless someone reached into our lives with the love of Christ. For me, that person was Tyler. Not a day goes by that I am not thankful for God using Tyler in my life. Tyler reached into my life, without partiality, to challenge me and ask if I truly understood who Christ was. Since that day, I now understand what the love of Christ is and what it means to not show partiality.

Who reached into your life? *My husband*
_____ *Andrew* _____
_____

Whose life do you need to reach into, without partiality? *as many as I can mainly my children*

As you continue with your week, I want to leave you with this challenge. Think of that person who you have been trying to reach or you know needs to be reached and start praying for them every day. Pray every day that God would give you the opportunity to reach into their lives in some capacity. Maybe it is by helping them move, by taking them out to eat, or visiting a loved one of theirs in the hospital. Pray for an opportunity. The Gospel of Christ is the most precious gift we have ever received. Therefore, as we are called to love our neighbors as ourselves, how can we not do all we can to reach those in need with His love and His amazing Gospel?

Reach / Devotion 1
RELATIONSHIP

Dr. Randy T. Johnson / *Growth Pastor*

"If my people who are called by my name humble themselves, and pray and seek my face and turn from their wicked ways, then I will hear from heaven and will forgive their sin and heal their land." 2 Chronicles 7:14

The United States of America needs Jesus. It was founded on Christian principles. God has blessed America. We need to make sure people do not rewrite the past ignoring our God. We also need to get our focus back on God. Pray for a revival.

Patrick Henry was one of the founding fathers of our country. He said, "It cannot be emphasized too strongly or too often that this great nation was founded, not by religionists, but by Christians not on religion, but on the gospel of Jesus Christ!" People do not need religion or a church. They need Jesus. It is not about religion; it is about a relationship with God Himself through Jesus Christ.

The Mayflower Compact, the Declaration of Independence, the U.S. Constitution, and Pledge of Allegiance all focus on the sovereign authority of God. It is not the sovereignty of the state or sovereignty of man. All 50 states mention God in their constitution. He is even referenced on our currency: In God We Trust!

Exodus 18:16 says, **"Whenever they have a dispute, it is brought to me, and I decide between the parties and inform them of God's decrees and instructions."** Moses knew he was not in charge. The government was not to be run by man's thoughts, but **"God's decrees and instructions."** When our thoughts differ from God's Word, we know who is wrong. Our country and our personal life need to focus on God's direction. When either chooses themselves instead, they break one of the Ten Commandments, **"You shall have no other gods before me"** (Exodus 20:3). We need to keep God on the throne of our life and pray our country will realize it too.

The Bible is clear that the government is still under God's control. Romans 13:1 says, **"Let everyone be subject to the governing authorities, for there is no authority except that which God has established. The authorities that exist have been established by God."** God set the government. He is still in control, but that does not mean our country can do whatever it wants and expect to be blessed. It is time for people to stop saying, "God bless America," and start saying, "America bless God." It needs to start with His children. We, as Christians, do not need just to step up and speak up; we need to drop to our knees.

Reach / Devotion 2

MORAL LAW

Dr. Randy T. Johnson / *Growth Pastor*

"If my people who are called by my name humble themselves, and pray and seek my face and turn from their wicked ways, then I will hear from heaven and will forgive their sin and heal their land." 2 Chronicles 7:14

The United States of America needs Jesus. It was founded on Christian principles. God has blessed America. We need to make sure people do not rewrite the past ignoring our God. We also need to get our focus back on God. Pray for a revival.

The sixth President of the United States, John Quincy Adams, said, "The highest glory of the American Revolution was this… it connected in one indissoluble bond the principles of civil government with the principles of Christianity."

Paragraph two of the Declaration of Independence famously starts, "We hold these truths to be self-evident, that all men are created equal, that they are endowed by their Creator with certain unalienable Rights, that among these are Life, Liberty and the pursuit of Happiness." Please catch the phrase, "truths to be self-evident." We are born with an innate sense of right and wrong. It lends itself to the idea of fixed standards and absolute truth.

C.S. Lewis argued for the existence of God based on this moral law in his book, Mere Christianity. It can be summarized as this:
1. There is a universal Moral Law.
2. If there is a universal Moral Law, there is a Moral Law-giver.
3. If there is a Moral Law-giver, it must be something beyond the universe.
4. Therefore, there is something beyond the universe.

Exodus 20 and Deuteronomy 5 both contain the Ten Commandments. Some have said Moses is the biggest sinner of all time because he broke all Ten Commandments in three seconds (remember, he threw the first set down because of the sin of the people, so God rewrote them). It is interesting to see that countries that do not have a copy of the Bible in their language already had a sense of what is right and what is wrong. Even the 1% biker gangs have a "set of rules." Moral Law exists.

Only a fool would say, "There are no absolutes" (as that is an absolute in itself). A friend of mine was in college when the professor said, "There are no absolutes." All he said in response was, "Absolutely." The professor scowled at him saying, "We are not going there." There are absolutes. There is truth. God's Word is the truth (John 17:17), and the truth will set us free (John 8:32).

As our country becomes more and more liberal, we need to hold to the truth. This age of tolerance weakens the mind as one is expected to believe that opposing theories are both right. Some things and thoughts are wrong. We need to share the truth in love. Mercy and truth are walking hand in hand.

Reach / Devotion 3
THREE BRANCHES
Dr. Randy T. Johnson / *Growth Pastor*

"If my people who are called by my name humble themselves, and pray and seek my face and turn from their wicked ways, then I will hear from heaven and will forgive their sin and heal their land." 2 Chronicles 7:14

The United States of America needs Jesus. It was founded on Christian principles. God has blessed America. We need to make sure people do not rewrite the past ignoring our God. We also need to get our focus back on God. Pray for a revival.

Jedidiah Morse was one of the founding fathers of the United States, and as a geographer, he wrote the first textbook on American geography. He made an interesting observation, "Whenever the pillars of Christianity shall be overthrown, our present form of government, and all blessings that flow from them, must fall with them." This is a scary thought, but it makes sense. If the foundation crumbles, the whole structure will collapse.

The Constitution created the three branches of government: Legislative, Judicial, and Executive branches. The Legislative branch makes the laws. The Judicial branch interprets the laws. The Executive branch enforces the laws. Have you ever wondered how our founding fathers came up with this three-fold approach?

Isaiah 33:22 says,
"For the Lord is our judge,
the Lord is our lawgiver,
the Lord is our king;
it is he who will save us."

This is a very clear description of our government: **"For the Lord is our judge** (Judicial branch)**, the Lord is our lawgiver** (Legislative branch)**, the Lord is our King** (Executive branch). I love the closing phrase, **"it is he who will save us."** It is the Lord who will save us. He has provided a structure to protect us and provide for us.

The Lord is our only hope. David says in Psalm 39:7, **"And now, O Lord, for what do I wait? My hope is in you."** Our hope remains in God. We are so fortunate for our country to be started by a group of people who feared God and based our government on God's Word. Jeremiah 29:11 is so comforting, **"For I know the plans I have for you, declares the Lord, plans for welfare and not for evil, to give you a future and a hope."** God wants to bless America. The United States needs to bless God. The foundation has been set. We cannot wait for others to make the change. Edmund Burke said it so well, "The only thing necessary for the triumph of evil is for good men to do nothing."

Reach / Devotion 4

GOT GOD?

Dr. Randy T. Johnson / *Growth Pastor*

George Washington made one of the most powerful statements I have ever heard, "It is impossible to govern the world without God and the Bible." That does not sound like separation of church and state. The government may not need the church, but President Washington understood it needed God and His Word. Romans 13:1 tells us that government was established by God, **"Let every person be subject to the governing authorities. For there is no authority except from God, and those that exist have been instituted by God."** The government is there to protect us; however, our salvation comes from God. Psalm 118:14 says, **"The Lord is my strength and my song; he has become my salvation."** We should not expect the government to be our strength or salvation.

The First Amendment reads, "Congress shall make no law respecting an establishment of religion, or prohibiting the free exercise thereof; or abridging the freedom of speech, or of the press; or the right of the people peaceably to assemble, and to petition the government for a redress of grievances." It was and is important to protect the church from the state. Our founding fathers knew they needed God and focused a lot of our laws and structure based on the Bible. There should be no strife between church and state.

1 Timothy 2:1-2 says, **"I urge, then, first of all, that petitions, prayers, intercession and thanksgiving be made for all people — for kings and all those in authority, that we may live peaceful and quiet lives in all godliness and holiness."** We need to pray for those in authority. It is not about political party; it is about God and His Word. These verses use some very key words: peaceful, quiet, godliness, and holiness. Peace and quiet are tied to morality

and character which is directed and orchestrated by the work of those in authority. The best way to support our authority is prayer. Prayer is so important the passage is almost redundant, "petitions, prayers, intercession and thanksgiving." We need to pray.

As a pastor, a very common phrase I hear is people at a funeral or going through a tragedy say, "I do not know how people who do not know God would get through this." God brings peace and direction. We need God; a key way to know God is His Word. As President Washington said, we need God and His Word.

"I entreat you in the most earnest manner to believe in Jesus Christ, for there is no salvation in any other [Acts 4:12]... If you are not reconciled to God through Jesus Christ, if you are not clothed with the spotless robe of His righteousness, you must forever perish." John Witherspoon, signer of the Declaration of Independence

Reach / Devotion 5
TAX EXEMPT
Dr. Randy T. Johnson / *Growth Pastor*

I do not know of anyone who likes to pay taxes. *Worldatlas* lists the countries with the highest taxes in the world. Ireland, Finland, United Kingdom, Japan, Austria, Belgium, and the Netherlands are all at about a 50% tax rate. Denmark and Sweden are about 55-56% with Aruba being the highest at close to 59%.

U.S. Code 501(c)(3) starts, "Corporations, and any community chest, fund, or foundation, organized and operated exclusively for religious, charitable, scientific, testing for public safety, literary, or educational purposes, or to foster national or international amateur sports competition…" This is part of the federal tax law and explains how churches are tax exempt.

It appears the Bible again came to mind. Ezra 7:24 says, **"You are also to know that you have no authority to impose taxes, tribute or duty on any of the priests, Levites, musicians, gatekeepers, temple servants or other workers at this house of God."** There were to be no taxes put on the house of God. Our country was founded on Christian principles. God has blessed America. We need to make sure people do not rewrite the past ignoring our God. We also need to get our focus back on God. Pray for a revival.

The Chief Justice of the United States is the presiding judge of the Supreme Court. The first Chief Justice was John Jay. He once said, "Providence has given to our people the choice of their rulers and it is the duty as well as the privilege and interest of a Christian nation to select and prefer Christians for their rulers." Is that not surprising? The Chief Justice told the people to vote for Christians. I think we, the church, bought into a separation of church and state and stopped encouraging our children to get into politics. America needs Christian lawyers, judges, representatives, congressmen, senators, and even Presidents. We need to pray. America needs Jesus.

In 1892, the Supreme Court stated, "Our laws and our institutions must necessarily be based upon and embody the teachings of the Redeemer of mankind. It's impossible that it should be otherwise; and to this extent our civilization and our institutions are emphatically Christian." I love the word, Redeemer. One of my favorite verses is Psalm 19:14, **"Let the words of my mouth and the meditation of my heart be acceptable in your sight, O Lord, my rock and my redeemer."** The Lord is our only Redeemer. We should want our thoughts, words, and actions to all be pleasing to Him.

Remember what we are told about the future. Job 19:25 says, **"For I know that my Redeemer lives, and at the last he will stand upon the earth."**

Jesus is coming back. He will rule!

Reach / Devotion 6
R E S P E C T
Dr. Randy T. Johnson / *Growth Pastor*

I was raised that there was crude talk and there was swearing. Neither were acceptable, but swearing was against God. In 1811, a man was caught using the name of Jesus Christ in vain. Not only did he swear, but he also started bad mouthing the Bible, too. The man was fined $500.00 and jailed for three months. His crime was blasphemy.

The court said if you have attacked Jesus Christ,
You have attacked Christianity.
If you attack Christianity,
You have attacked the foundation of the U.S.
Therefore, it is an attack on the U.S.

In this case of People vs. Ruggles, the court said, "Whatever strikes at the root of Christianity tends manifestly to the dissolution of civil government." To go against God was (and hopefully is) synonymous with going against our country. The United States has such a godly heritage. We have been blessed.

The Bible is clear about how we talk. We need to show respect in how we use the name of the Lord. We should not use it in vain or even in a flippant way. The Ten Commandments are listed in Exodus 20. The third commandment says, **"You shall not take the name of the Lord your God in vain, for the Lord will not hold him guiltless who takes his name in vain"** (verse 7). We see it recorded again in Deuteronomy 5:10-11, "**But showing steadfast love to thousands of those who love me and keep my commandments. You shall not take the name of the Lord your God in vain, for the Lord will not hold him guiltless who takes his name in vain.**" Both passages make it clear that those who use God's name in vain, will be punished. They will be guilty as charged.

Psalm 139:19-20 adds insight into the topic, **"Oh that you would slay the wicked, O God! O men of blood, depart from me! They speak against you with malicious intent; your enemies take your name in vain."** Those who use the name of the Lord in vain are viewed as His enemy. God does not take our words lightly.

Matthew 12:36-37 takes our words and careless words to a whole new level, **"I tell you, on the day of judgment people will give account for every careless word they speak, for by your words you will be justified, and by your words you will be condemned."**

Be careful what you say, not only can it be held against you in the court of law, it can be held against you in the day of judgment. Do not just stop saying inappropriate things, but speak mercy and truth. Ephesians 4:29-30 says, **"Let no corrupting talk come out of your mouths, but only such as is good for building up, as fits the occasion, that it may give grace to those who hear. And do not grieve the Holy Spirit of God, by whom you were sealed for the day of redemption."**

07 / *Jen Combs,
Wife of Lead Pastor Josh Combs*

GATHER

Sunday. What feeling do you get most often when you hear that word? _____
_____

Stress? Guilt? Dread? Tired? Inconvenienced? Bored? Notice I said most often because there are certainly some Sundays I feel those things. I am not a fan of the guy that wrote, "It is easy like Sunday morning." I want to throat punch him. He apparently did not attend gatherings and have to get seven people out the door. But in all seriousness, if you feel those things every week, you might want to check your relationship with Jesus. You see, Sunday is the day we choose to gather as believers. The definition of gather is to come together, assemble, or bring together and take in from scattered places. If you have ever listened to a sermon from my husband you for sure would have heard him say this statement, "We do not go to church, we are the church." It is safe to say I would be a millionaire if I had a penny for every time I have heard him say this. I also must confess; I have probably given him an equal amount of eye rolls. But I digress. It is so true. That is precisely why we do not say, "Oh I am going to church. Or oh, we have church services." Both of those things point to the church being a performance or a specific place we attend. In 1 Corinthians 12:27 it says, **"Now you are the body of Christ and individually members of it."**

Now that we are clear on who the church is (believers!), it is important to figure out what we are supposed to do. Hebrews 10:25 says, **"Not** _forsaking_ **the** _assembling_ **of** _ourselves_ **together, as the** _manner_ **of some, but** _exhorting_ **one** _another_ **."**

We are supposed to meet together or gather. Remember earlier our definition said bringing together and taking from scattered places.

During the week the Lord scatters us to our stations to serve Him. 1 Corinthians 7:17 says, **"Only let each person lead the life that the Lord has assigned to him, and to which God has called him."** Acts 8:4 adds, **"Now those who were scattered went about preaching the word."** God has you right where He wants you during the week, at your set station, to further the Gospel.

What are you doing at your station to further the Gospel?
_____
_____
_____

What should you be doing that you are not already doing?
_____
_____
_____

So what should our gatherings look like? _____
_____
_____

1. Gatherings are meant to be like the coach gathering all of his players together to give them a talk before he sends them back out into the game. Sometimes that talk is a pep talk, and sometimes that talk is a warning of things to change. 2 Timothy 4:1-2 says it this way, **"I charge you in the presence of God and of Christ Jesus, who is to judge the living and the dead, and by his appearing and his kingdom: preach the word; be ready in season and out of season; reprove, rebuke, and exhort, with complete patience and teaching."**

What are we supposed to listen to at a gathering? _____
_____
_____

2. Ephesians 5:19 says, "*Addressing one another in psalms and hymns and spiritual songs, singing and making a melody to the Lord with your heart.*" Psalm 98:4 adds, "*Make a joyful noise to the Lord, all the earth; break forth into joyous song and sing praise.*"

According to these passages, what are we supposed to do when we gather? _____ Sing _____
_____
_____

Since we need to be honest, we do not all sound so great when those joyful noises are coming out of our mouths (this includes me!) I have just learned to get a front row seat next to the speakers so I can belt it out to Jesus and no one but He has to hear me.

3. 2 Corinthians 8:1-5 says, "*We want you to know, brothers, about the grace of God that has been given among the churches of Macedonia, for in a severe test of affliction, their abundance of joy and their extreme poverty have overflowed in a wealth of generosity on their part. For they gave according to their means, as I can testify, and beyond their means, of their own accord, begging us earnestly for the favor of taking part in the relief of saints and this, not as we expected, but they gave of themselves first to the Lord and then by the will of God to us.*"

According to 2 Corinthians, what else is supposed to be a part of our gathering? _____
_____
_____

Are you participating in this kind of worship? _____
_____
_____

4. In John 12:26 Jesus says, **"If anyone serves me, he must follow me; and where I am, there will my servant be also. If anyone serves me, the Father will honor him."**

What else is supposed to be a part of our worship? _____
_____
_____

Where are you currently serving? Where has the Holy Spirit been whispering to you to start serving? Let me just give you a hint; there are tons of areas all around that need you. It may be in the nursery, with the children, or in the student ministry. Should you help with building or cleaning around the church buildings? Can you cook a meal? Will you write cards? Are you mechanical and could work on buses? Should you help take the offering? Would you like to help mow the grass? Would you be willing to empty the trash? Do you play an instrument? Are you willing to make coffee? Would you stack chairs? This is just a starter list. Get in contact with your Connection Pastor or your Growth Community leader, and we will welcome your teamwork. Remember, you are the church.

5. 1 Thessalonians 5:11 says, **"Therefore encourage one another and build one another up, just as you are doing."**

What does 1 Thessalonians say we should do? _____
_____
_____

How are you encouraging others? _____
_____
_____

When we come and gather together, it is supposed to be an active time. It is not just somewhere you attend, sit down, check a box, and leave. If you truly are a follower of Christ, you are going to want to be actively involved in a gathering and all throughout the week. If you are not and you dread all that we talked about on a consistent basis, you need to do some chatting with Jesus and see how you can be His and how to love Him as your Lord. If you need help with this at all, please contact any one of our staff or your Growth Community leader. Do not forget to be listening to sermons, singing in worship, giving, serving, and encouraging one another.

Gather / Devotion 1

SCHOOLING

Dr. Randy T. Johnson / *Growth Pastor*

"*If my people who are called by my name humble themselves, and pray and seek my face and turn from their wicked ways, then I will hear from heaven and will forgive their sin and heal their land.*" 2 Chronicles 7:14

The United States of America needs Jesus. It was founded on Christian principles. God has blessed America. We need to make sure people do not rewrite the past ignoring our God. We also need to get our focus back on God. Pray for a revival.

The Bible was important to our founding fathers. In a ten-year study undertaken at the University of Houston, researchers examined 15,000 documents from America's founders and determined that:
- 34% of their quotations came directly from the Bible,
- 94% of their quotes were based on the Bible,
- 60% used the Bible to arrive at their conclusion.

The founding fathers studied, knew, and applied the Word of God. They knew it was important and that the Bible changed lives. Scripture became a part of primary and basic steps in the formation of our country. The Northwest Ordinance makes sure that children gain an appreciation for God and His Word. Section 14 Article 3 starts, "Religion, morality, and knowledge, being necessary to good government and the happiness of mankind, schools and the means of education shall forever be encouraged." New areas needed to have schools. Those schools needed to incorporate religion, morality, and knowledge. Schooling is not just to be of the mind. It needs to involve the heart and soul of our children.

Religious education was encouraged. This is not about whether our kids should go to Christian, private, parochial, or public school. It is not whether or not they should be homeschooled. It is that our children need to be taught the Bible and character development. Deuteronomy 6:4-7 says, **"Hear, O Israel: The Lord our God, the Lord is one. Love the Lord your God with all your heart and with all your soul and with all your strength. These commandments that I give you today are to be on your hearts. Impress them on your children. Talk about them when you sit at home and when you walk along the road, when you lie down and when you get up."** We are responsible for teaching our children about God and His Word. It needs to be a natural and intentional part of our lives.

Ephesians 6:4 adds, **"Fathers, do not exasperate your children; instead, bring them up in the training and instruction of the Lord."** Our homes, our schooling, and our country need Jesus. Our leadership, our children, and each of us need Jesus. Be intentional. Pray specifically.

George Washington said, "What students would learn in American schools above all is the religion of Jesus Christ." Benjamin Franklin insisted that schools should teach "the excellency of the Christian religion above all others, ancient or modern."

Gather / Devotion 2
EQUALITY
Dr. Randy T. Johnson / *Growth Pastor*

The Constitution of the United States' First Amendment says, "Congress shall make no law respecting an establishment of religion or prohibiting the free exercise thereof…" From the start, the goal of our founding fathers was to protect the church from the state. It was not to keep them separate or to protect the state from the church. Psalm 33:12 says it so well, **"Blessed is the nation whose God is the Lord, the people he chose for his inheritance."** Our nation, government, legal system, and authorities need God. It is God who blesses and who withholds blessings.

There were twelve pre-draft variations of the Constitution, which are all expressed in the sentiments found in this one, "Congress will pass no laws making one denomination of Christians higher than another denomination." It is interesting that it does not say religion; it says denomination. By definition, all denominations hold to Jesus being God, while religions vary. Our country was not founded on the choice of any religion; it was based on Christianity.

Another concept that shows our Christian heritage is how the founding fathers viewed all men as being created equal. The second paragraph of the Declaration of Independence says, "We hold these truths to be self-evident, that all men are created equal, that they are endowed by their Creator with certain unalienable Rights, that among these are Life, Liberty and the pursuit of Happiness." All men are created equal. Realize the theistic aspect of the reference to people being created and God being referenced as the Creator. That is awesome. God is the creator. You were created by Him and therefore have value, meaning, and purpose.

All men being created equal was not a new concept. Our founding fathers would have found this in the Bible. Acts 10:34 says, **"Then Peter began to speak: 'I now realize how true it is that God does not show favoritism.'"** As Americans, we probably cannot fully appreciate the depth of this concept. God treats us all the same and our government was set up to treat all people the same.

Galatians 3:28 also reminds us, **"There is neither Jew nor Gentile, neither slave nor free, nor is there male and female, for you are all one in Christ Jesus."** We are all equal in Christ. There is no favoritism. God loves you no matter what your gender, color, race, height, width, and personality portrait. We are all the same. We all need Jesus.

"He who made all men hath made the truths necessary to human happiness obvious to all... Our forefathers opened the Bible to all." Samuel Adams, signer of the Declaration of Independence.

Gather / Devotion 3
P E O P L E R U L E

Dr. Randy T. Johnson / *Growth Pastor*

The Founders of the Constitution said, "The great vital and conservative element in our system is the belief of our people in the pure doctrine and divine truths of the gospel of Jesus Christ." They sincerely held to the Gospel of Jesus Christ. It is a shame that I might sound politically incorrect or intolerant to quote our founding fathers. We cannot let history be rewritten.

An aspect I like about our government is that there was an importance placed on governing self and family as the first level of governance. This can be seen in several of the Amendments to the Constitution.

- The First Amendment says, "Congress shall make no law respecting an establishment of religion, or prohibiting the free exercise thereof; or abridging the freedom of speech, or of the press; or the right of the people peaceably to assemble, and to petition the Government for a redress of grievances." This Amendment shows a trust in people. People are to work things out together peaceably and go to the Government as the last option, not the first.
- The Second Amendment adds, "A well regulated Militia, being necessary to the security of a free State, the right of the people to keep and bear Arms, shall not be infringed." Again people are to settle issues and not expect the Government to handle everything.
- The Ninth Amendment continues the thought, "The enumeration in the Constitution, of certain rights, shall not be construed to deny or disparage others retained by the people." People are the focus, not the Government.
- The Tenth Amendment also says, "The powers not delegated to the United States by the Constitution, nor prohibited by it to the States, are reserved to the States respectively, or to the people." Power is delegated to people. We need to figure out how to live together.

This concept of people going to each other first is clear in Scripture. Matthew 18:15-17 says, **"If your brother or sister sins, go and point out their fault, just between the two of you. If they listen to you, you have won them over. But if they will not listen, take one or two others along, so that 'every matter may be established by the testimony of two or three witnesses.' If they still refuse to listen, tell it to the church; and if they refuse to listen even to the church, treat them as you would a pagan or a tax collector."** When wronged, we are encouraged to go to the person, not the court.

1 Corinthians 6:1 discourages us in taking others to court. It says, **"When one of you has a grievance against another, does he dare go to law before the unrighteous instead of the saints?"** Suing is not to be the first option. We need to try and settle things outside of the court.

Our country was founded on Christian principles with an emphasis to live correctly. The founders emphasized "pure doctrine and divine truths of the gospel of Jesus Christ." We are blessed and need to be a blessing to God.

Gather / Devotion 4
TEN COMMANDMENTS
Dr. Randy T. Johnson / *Growth Pastor*

In 1980 it became illegal to post the Ten Commandments in schools. We as a nation have fallen so far. James Madison said, "We have staked the whole future of American civilization not upon the power of government, far from it. We have staked the future of all our political institutions upon the capacity of each and all of us to govern ourselves according to the Ten Commandments of God." Madison knew the value of God's Law. Here is the list from Exodus 20 and Deuteronomy 5:

1. You shall have no other gods before Me.
2. You shall make no idols.
3. You shall not take the name of the Lord your God in vain.
4. Keep the Sabbath day holy.
5. Honor your father and your mother.
6. You shall not murder.
7. You shall not commit adultery.
8. You shall not steal.
9. You shall not bear false witness against your neighbor.
10. You shall not covet.

Which of those is offensive? Why would we not want those posted in every school?

The removal of the Ten Commandments was not the only major lapse in judgment of our government.
- 1963 – Removal of prayer from schools.
- 1963 – Removal of Bible reading in schools.
- 1965 – Removal of religious instruction in schools.
- 1965 – Illegal for a student to pray aloud in schools.

There is a spiritual war all around us. Ephesians 6 talks about the armor of God. Look how verse 6 describes the battle, **"For we do not wrestle against flesh and blood, but against the rulers, against the authorities, against the cosmic powers over this present darkness, against the spiritual forces of evil in the heavenly places."** Our battle is not between political parties. It is with Satan. He does not want our children reading the Bible or talking with God. He does not like it when people do things for or with God. Misery loves company and Satan wants to take down anyone and everyone he can.

> 2 Corinthians 10:3-5 says, *"For though we walk in the flesh, we are not waging war according to the flesh. For the weapons of our warfare are not of the flesh but have divine power to destroy strongholds. We destroy arguments and every lofty opinion raised against the knowledge of God, and take every thought captive to obey Christ."*

Put on the armor of God and protect our godly heritage. Protect our past, present, and future. Protect our country.

James Madison is very clear in saying, "We've staked our future on our ability to follow the Ten Commandments with all of our heart." He also said, "We have staked the whole future of American civilization, not upon the power of government, far from it. We've staked the future of all our political institutions upon our capacity...to sustain ourselves according to the Ten Commandments of God."

Gather / Devotion 5

JUSTICE AND MORALITY

Dr. Randy T. Johnson / *Growth Pastor*

John Adams said, "We have no government armed with power capable of contending with human passions unbridled by morality and religion. Our constitution was made only for a moral and religious people. It is whole inadequate to the government of any other." I am thrilled to read about men of old who influenced our lives today. President Adams understood the importance of doing the right thing. It is interesting he did not just say morality. He understood that morality is not enough in itself, it needs to be God focused. He emphasized religion because he wanted to make sure we remembered how we become clean. It is only through God and the Gospel of Jesus Christ that we can truly live right.

The purpose of our government was to establish justice. The Bible addresses this issue. Leviticus 19:15 says, **"Do not pervert justice; do not show partiality to the poor or favoritism to the great, but judge your neighbor fairly."** It is sad that we need to be reminded that we should be fair and honest. God knew favoritism would be a problem. The command is repeated in Deuteronomy 1:17, **"Do not show partiality in judging; hear both small and great alike. Do not be afraid of anyone, for judgment belongs to God. Bring me any case too hard for you, and I will hear it."** God gives guidelines for administering justice, but He also reminds us that He is the Ultimate Judge. God will judge, and we need to rule carefully today.

In governing the country, the people understood that they were God's servants. Romans 13:4 says, **"For the one in authority is God's servant for your good. But if you do wrong, be afraid, for rulers do not bear the sword for no reason. They are**

God's servants, agents of wrath to bring punishment on the wrongdoer." Twice the phrase **"God's servants"** is used. It is clear that God is emphasizing an important concept to us. They are from God and should operate on behalf of God.

When people understand the Golden Rule, **"So whatever you wish that others would do to you, do also to them"** (Matthew 7:14), it covers most of the laws. Do unto others as you would want them to do to you is a great mission statement for our lives.

Have a proper mindset. Judge and rule fairly. Live humbly.

"If we abide by the principles taught in the Bible, our country will go on prospering and to prosper; but if we and our posterity neglect its instruction and authority, no man can tell how sudden a catastrophe may overwhelm us and bury all our glory in profound obscurity."
Daniel Webster

Gather / Devotion 6

WITNESSES

Dr. Randy T. Johnson / *Growth Pastor*

Ben Franklin said, "We need God to be our friend not our enemy. We need Him to be our ally not our adversary. We need to make sure we keep God's concurring aid. If a sparrow cannot fall without God's notice, how can our nation rise without His aid?" This is so powerful and right on track. We need God to be our friend. We do not want to fight with Him. I like how Franklin referenced Matthew 10:29-33 when he speaks of the sparrows, **"Are not two sparrows sold for a penny? And not one of them will fall to the ground apart from your Father. But even the hairs of your head are all numbered. Fear not, therefore; you are of more value than many sparrows."**

Franklin referenced the Bible and acknowledged that God is always watching us and that He sees everything. The Bible was used for illustrations, but more importantly, it was used to help develop our country. The Sixth Amendment addresses the topic of having a fair trial with witnesses, "In all criminal prosecutions, the accused shall enjoy the right to a speedy and public trial, by an impartial jury of the State and district wherein the crime shall have been committed, which district shall have been previously ascertained by law, and to be informed of the nature and cause of the accusation; to be confronted with the witnesses against him; to have compulsory process for obtaining witnesses in his favor, and to have the Assistance of Counsel for his defence."

The concept of having witnesses and a fair trial is clearly seen in Deuteronomy 19:15, **"One witness is not enough to convict anyone accused of any crime or offense they may have committed. A matter must be established by the testimony of two or three witnesses."** One person cannot frame another on his statement alone. There needs to be at least another witness. Matthew 18:16 also talks about having witnesses, **"But if they will not listen, take one or two others along, so that 'every matter may be established by the testimony of two or three witnesses.'"** These verses remind us that the first course of action is not to go to court; it is to go to the person.

John Quincy Adams also expressed his sentiments about God's Word when he said, "The first and almost only book deserving of universal attention is the Bible. I speak as a man of the world...and I say to you, 'Search the Scriptures.'"

Our founding fathers were followers of God and strived to live by His Word. Our country was founded on godly principles. We are blessed because of it.

08 / Philip Piasecki,
Worship Leader

GROW

Grow

The concept of growth is incredible when you stop and think about it. Take a second to think about a seed. When a seed is planted, with the proper care, it can grow into a majestic tree. It grows from a seed that can be held between two fingers, to a tree that can tower over buildings. Think about a baby, who first grows in his mother's womb, and then after being born continues to grow and develop in miraculous ways. The concept of growth is something that we can become so numb to; we see it every day, so we take it for granted. When we stop to appreciate it, we can see God working in the midst of creation each and every day.

What are some "simple, everyday" often overlooked ways you see God working? _remember small things_

Not only does God cause physical growth, but He also causes spiritual growth inside of us. When we become believers in Christ, that is the beginning of our spiritual growth. At that point in our lives, God compares us to babies who need milk. We were never meant to stay spiritual babies; we are supposed to grow into full grown spiritual adults. My daughter, Molly, is a cute baby, but if she suddenly stopped physically growing as she got older, we would have a serious problem! When we give our lives to Christ, there should be a desire within us to get to know Him better; we should not be satisfied where we are at spiritually. Psalm 1 further explores this concept of spiritual growth.

> Psalm 1:1-3 - *"Blessed is the man who walks not in the counsel of the wicked, nor stands in the way of sinners, nor sits in the seat of scoffers; but his delight is in the law of the Lord, and on his law he meditates day and night. He is like a tree planted*

by streams of water that yields its fruit in its season, and its leaf does not wither. In all that he does, he prospers."

What are some things you can do to grow spiritually? _____
lessons, bible study, pray

Throughout Scripture, a believer's spiritual life is compared to a tree. We see here in Psalm 1 that someone who meditates on the Word of God and surrounds himself with godly people is compared to a tree planted by streams of water. This tree produces fruit, which is a byproduct of it being a healthy tree.

Why is it so important that you grow spiritually? _____

Is your spiritual walk more mature than it was when you were first saved? Five years ago? One year ago? _____
should be

Spiritual growth is a sign of a healthy Christian. If you are seeking after the things of Christ like you are supposed to be, then you will see growth in your life. Throughout your Christian walk, you may find yourself growing at different rates depending on the spiritual season you are experiencing. But if you look back to the day you gave your life to Christ, and cannot significantly identify differences in your spiritual life then that is an issue. If you are not growing spiritually, and you are not producing fruit, it could be a sign of a much greater problem.

Grow

What are some symptoms of a healthy Christian? _____
_____
_____

What are some symptoms of an unhealthy Christian? _____
_____
_____

> Matthew 7:17-19 says, "*So, every healthy tree bears good fruit, but the diseased tree bears bad fruit. A healthy tree cannot bear bad fruit, nor can a diseased tree bear good fruit. Every tree that does not bear good fruit is cut down and thrown into the fire.*"
>
> Matthew 7:21-23 goes on to say, "*Not everyone who says to me, 'Lord, Lord,' will enter the kingdom of heaven, but the one who does the will of my Father who is in heaven. On that day many will say to me, 'Lord, Lord, did we not prophesy in your name, and cast out demons in your name, and do many mighty works in your name?' And then will I declare to them, 'I never knew you; depart from me, you workers of lawlessness.'*"

What are your thoughts on the warnings of these verses? _____
_____
_____

These verses are so haunting to read, and I feel like many Christians want to avoid reading Scripture with this message. The sad truth is that there are many people who believe they are going to Heaven, that are going to be tragically disappointed when they come face to face with Christ. 2 Corinthians 2:17 tells us that anyone who is in Christ that he is a new creation! If you truly are a new creation, this means that your life should look different than it did before Christ.

Galatians 5:22-25 shows the fruit that your life should be producing if you are truly in Christ, **"But the fruit of the Spirit is love, joy, peace, patience, kindness, goodness, faithfulness, gentleness, self-control; against such things there is no law. And those who belong to Christ Jesus have crucified the flesh with its passions and desires. If we live by the Spirit, let us also keep in step with the Spirit."**

What part of the Fruit of the Spirit do you feel is strongest in your life? _____

_____

_____

What part of the Fruit of the Spirit do you feel is the weakest in your life? _____

_____

_____

The Fruit of the Spirit is a way to measure your spiritual walk. These traits should be evident in some way in your life, and you should always desire for these things to grow stronger in your life as well. Believers should be the most loving people on this earth. Every believer can look at this list and identify areas where he or she needs to be better. We need to love people as Christ has loved us, we need to live at peace with others, we need to show patience and kindness to others, we need to have faith in the things of Christ, we need to be gentle and have self-control in our lives. The only way we can do these things are through the power of Christ through His Holy Spirit.

Why are some of these traits so difficult to produce in our lives?

free Will
don't trust the
truth, emotions

Your salvation is not something of which you have to constantly worry. If you confessed that Christ is Lord of your life, and repented from your sins, then you are a child of God. Now it is time to start producing fruit in your life. Do not be satisfied where you are currently at in your relationship with Christ. It should be your desire to become more like Christ each day. Seek Him each day through prayer and reading His Word. Spend time studying the Word with other believers and discussing the Word of God. Spend time worshiping Him through song and your actions. When you do these things, you will produce fruit just like a tree planted by streams of water.

Grow / Devotion 1
KING OF KINGS

Dr. Randy T. Johnson / *Growth Pastor*

"If my people who are called by my name humble themselves, and pray and seek my face and turn from their wicked ways, then I will hear from heaven and will forgive their sin and heal their land." 2 Chronicles 7:14

In 1796 the court made a statement, "In our form of government the Christian religion is the established religion and all sects and denominations of Christians are placed upon the same equal footing." The court openly stated that our country was based on the Christian faith.

It should be noted that the Republican form of government was necessary. They regularly gave warnings against kings for godly rulers. The Constitution of the United States laid the foundation against being ruled by an earthly king. The founders made clear statements. When Samuel Adams signed the Declaration of Independence in 1776, he said, "We have this day restored the King to whom all men ought to be obedient. He reigns in heaven and from the rising to the setting of the sun, let His kingdom come." Jesus is the King of kings.

Revelation 17:14 refers to Jesus as King, **"They will make war on the Lamb, and the Lamb will conquer them, for he is Lord of lords and King of kings, and those with him are called and chosen and faithful." Revelation 19:16 adds, "On his robe and on his thigh he has a name written, King of kings and Lord of lords."** John Adams and John Hancock stated, "We recognize no Sovereign but God, and no King but Jesus!"

In Exodus 18:21 Moses knew that it was not part of God's will for them to have a king, **"But select capable men from all the people — men who fear God, trustworthy men who hate dishonest gain — and appoint them as officials over thousands, hundreds, fifties and tens."** It was not to be a one-man show. Proverbs 11:14 adds, **"For lack of guidance a nation falls, but victory is won through many advisers."** Finally, Proverbs 24:6 also says, **"Surely you need guidance to wage war, and victory is won through many advisers."**

The United States has a set of checks and balances that should not be controlled by one man or person. We need Jesus. It was founded on Christian principles. God has blessed America. We need to make sure people do not rewrite the past ignoring our God. We also need to get our focus back on God. Pray for a revival.

Grow / Devotion 2

FREE INDEED

Dr. Randy T. Johnson / *Growth Pastor*

French writer Alexis de Tocqueville, after visiting America in 1831 said, "I sought for the greatness and genius of America in her commodious harbors and her ample rivers — and it was not there... in her fertile fields and bound less forests — and it was not there... in her rich mines and her vast world commerce — and it was not there... in her democratic Congress and her matchless Constitution — and it was not there. Not until I went into the churches of America and heard her pulpits flame with righteousness did I understand the secret of her genius and power. America is great because she is good, and if America ever ceases to be good, she will cease to be great."

America is beautiful because she is good. She is good because she is founded on Christian principles. Our freedom is based on biblical liberty. The Bible has a lot to say about freedom and liberty. John 8:36 says, **"So if the Son sets you free, you will be free indeed."** True freedom comes through Jesus Christ. Everyone is trapped by sin, but the death of Jesus gave us the opportunity to be free. You can be free indeed. It can be an interesting wordplay to realize that the goodness that comes from Jesus makes us free indeed and even free in deed. We now have the freedom to do what is right. We can do good deeds. We are not full of sin.

The goodness that was noticed by Alexis de Tocqueville comes through Jesus. Galatians 5:1 adds, **"It is for freedom that Christ has set us free. Stand firm, then, and do not let yourselves be burdened again by a yoke of slavery."** Sin and guilt can hold us back or down, but forgiveness through Christ sets us free. We have genuine freedom. We no longer have to be burdened by sin. Sin enslaves us, but Jesus releases us.

1 Peter 2:16 reminds us of our freedom, **"Live as free people, but do not use your freedom as a cover-up for evil; live as God's slaves."** We need to think and act like people who are freed from the bondage of sin. As our godly heritage is mocked and rewritten, we need to take a stand. I am nervous for the next generation because of the quote by Dr. William James, the Father of Modern Psychology, when he said, "There is nothing so absurd but if you repeat it often enough, people will believe it." The media is so anti-Christian that it repeatedly lies about our heritage. People are starting to believe it. Our country has been blessed by God. God does not owe us anything. Thomas Jefferson said, "Indeed, I tremble for my country when I reflect that God is just, that His justice cannot sleep forever." We, the Church, need to humble ourselves, repent, and pray for God's mercy and grace.

Edmund Burke said, "All that is necessary for the triumph of evil is that good men do nothing."

Grow / Devotion 3

CREATOR AND SAVIOR

Dr. Randy T. Johnson / *Growth Pastor*

The United States of America was founded on the Gospel of Jesus Christ. There is a myriad of quotations available stating a strong position for Christianity. The emphasis was not freedom of religion as much as it was the necessity to keep God in the forefront. Ben Franklin said, "Introduce into public affairs the principles of Christianity and it will change the face of the world." Jesus changes lives. Our country needs that change. We need Jesus.

John Witherspoon, a signer of the Declaration of Independence, said, "I entreat you in the most earnest manner to believe in Jesus Christ, for there is no salvation in any other (Acts 4:12)... If you are not reconciled to God through Jesus Christ, if you are not clothed with the spotless robe of His righteousness, you must forever perish." Witherspoon is very pointed in his statement. He believed there is a Heaven and a Hell. The difference in the destination is what you do with Jesus. He also said, "Christ Jesus — the promise of old made unto the fathers, the hope of Israel (Acts 28:20), the light of the world (John 8:12), and the end of the law for righteousness to every one that believeth (Romans 10:4) — is the only Savior of sinners, in opposition to all false religions and every uninstituted rite; as He Himself says (John 14:6): 'I am the way, and the truth, and the life: no man cometh unto the Father but by Me.'" It is impressive on how many verses he referenced. He understood Scripture. He knew the Gospel. He wanted our country to be Christian.

Although our founding fathers were grounded in Christianity, today the battle seems to be if God exists. This was not their fight. They knew and spoke of the Creator. The second paragraph of the

Declaration of Independence starts, "We hold these truths to be self-evident, that all men are created equal, that they are endowed by their Creator with certain unalienable Rights, that among these are Life, Liberty and the pursuit of Happiness." They used the words 'created' and 'Creator.' There was not even a hint of evolution being believed, much less taught in the schools. They knew the Bible and apparently the very first verse of God's Word, **"In the beginning God created the heavens and the earth."**

Charles Finney gave an appropriate challenge, "The church must take right ground in regard to politics. Politics are part of religion in a country as this, and Christians must do their duty to the country as a part of their duty to God. He will bless or curse this nation according to the course Christians take in politics."

Grow / Devotion 4

WILL WORK 4 FOOD

Dr. Randy T. Johnson / *Growth Pastor*

Noah Webster said, "The moral principles and precepts contained in the scriptures ought to form the basis of all our civil constitutions and laws. All the miseries and evils which men suffer from vice, crime, ambition, injustice, oppression, slavery, and war, proceed from their despising or neglecting the precepts contained in the Bible." He realized how powerful, complete, at practical the Word of God is. A lot of our restitution laws are based on Numbers 5:5-7, **"The Lord said to Moses, 'Say to the Israelites: 'Any man or woman who wrongs another in any way and so is unfaithful to the Lord is guilty and must confess the sin they have committed. They must make full restitution for the wrong they have done, add a fifth of the value to it and give it all to the person they have wronged.'"** Clear advice and instruction are given.

America has been blessed financially. In his last will and testament, Patrick Henry added a nice twist to the concept, "This is all the inheritance I can give my dear family. The religion of Christ can give them one which will make them rich indeed." Our country was founded by men who understood the Gospel and wanted it passed down for generations. They started our nation on the principles found in the Bible.

The economic structure of America has always been biblical capitalism. If you want to eat, then work. If you do not work, you will not eat. 2 Thessalonians 3:6-15 says, **"In the name of the Lord Jesus Christ, we command you, brothers and sisters, to keep away from every believer who is idle and disruptive and does not live according to the teaching you received from us. For** *you yourselves know how you ought to follow our example. We were not idle when we were with you, nor did we eat anyone's food without paying for it. On the contrary, we worked night and day, laboring and toiling so that we would not be a burden to any of you. We did this, not because we do not have the right to such help, but in order to offer ourselves as a model for you to imitate. For even when we were with you, we gave you this rule: 'The one who is unwilling to work shall not eat.' We hear that some among you are idle and disruptive. They are not busy; they are busybodies. Such people we command and urge in the Lord Jesus Christ to settle down and earn the food they eat. And as for you, brothers and sisters, never tire of doing what is good. Take special note of anyone who does not obey our instruction in this letter. Do not associate with them, in order that they may feel ashamed. Yet do not regard them as an enemy, but warn them as you would a fellow believer."* Paul accounts for his work ethic. He expected others to do the same.

Alan Greenspan said, "Capitalism is based on self-interest and self-esteem; it holds integrity and trustworthiness as cardinal virtues and makes them pay off in the marketplace, thus demanding that men survive by means of virtue, not vices. It is this superlatively moral system that the welfare statists propose to improve upon by means of preventative law, snooping bureaucrats, and the chronic goad of fear."

All political systems rely on integrity. There needs to be morality and virtue. This goodness can only come through a relationship with Jesus Christ. We then receive the Holy Spirit and can be directed to do right for all and to all.

Grow / Devotion 5

WE ARE FAMILY

Dr. Randy T. Johnson / *Growth Pastor*

John Adams said, "We have no government armed with power capable of contending with human passions unbridled by morality and religion. Avarice, ambition, revenge, or gallantry, would break the strongest cords of our Constitution as a whale goes through a net. Our Constitution was made only for a moral and religious people. It is wholly inadequate to the government of any other." The United States was designed with morality in mind. Our founding fathers knew of the importance of the traditional family structure. Number five of the Ten Commandments says, **"Honor your father and your mother, so that you may live long in the land the Lord your God is giving you"** (Exodus 20:12). The family is important. It is a God-designed institution. It is so important that our government designed some laws based around it.

Throughout our country's history, they have strived to protect and provide for the family. You could see this in tax exemptions, but also in the concept of holding the family together. Divorce takes time, money, and energy. There have been few acceptable reasons for divorce, and still, it took time. Our country has not taken marriage lightly. Exodus 20:14 reports another one of the Ten Commandments, **"You shall not commit adultery."** The idea was not new to our country, yet was important. In Mark 10:2-12 the question of divorce is raised to Jesus, **"Some Pharisees came and tested him by asking, 'Is it lawful for a man to divorce his wife?' 'What did Moses command you?' he replied. They said, 'Moses permitted a man to write a certificate of divorce and send her away.' 'It was because your hearts were hard that Moses wrote you this law,' Jesus replied. 'But at the beginning of creation God 'made them male and female.' 'For this reason** *a man will leave his father and mother and be united to his wife, and the two will become one flesh.' So they are no longer two, but one flesh. Therefore what God has joined together, let no one separate.' When they were in the house again, the disciples asked Jesus about this. He answered, 'Anyone who divorces his wife and marries another woman commits adultery against her. And if she divorces her husband and marries another man, she commits adultery.'"*

The Bible and our country have historically held to the traditional family structure. It was passed on for generations and derived from God's Word. The Bible was always pivotal for the founding fathers. Although not a founding father, President Dwight D. Eisenhower agreed with this concept when he said, "The Bible is endorsed by the ages. Our civilization is built upon its words. In no other book is there such a collection of inspired wisdom, reality, and hope."

> *"You shall love the Lord your God with all your heart and with all your soul and with all your might. And these words that I command you today shall be on your heart. You shall teach them diligently to your children, and shall talk of them when you sit in your house, and when you walk by the way, and when you lie down, and when you rise"* (Deuteronomy 6:5-7).

Grow / Devotion 6

GOD'S SERVANT

Dr. Randy T. Johnson / *Growth Pastor*

Dinesh D'Souza makes an interesting observation about government and leadership, "Christianity enhanced the notion of political and social accountability by providing a new model: that of servant leadership. In ancient Greece and Rome no one would have dreamed of considering political leaders anyone's servants. The job of the leader was to lead. But Christ invented the notion that the way to lead is by serving the needs of others, especially those who are the neediest. Mark 10:43 quotes Christ: 'Whoever wants to become great among you must be your servant... for even the Son of Man did not come to be served but to serve.'" Jesus was the greatest leader of all time and was the most excellent servant. For Him, they went together naturally.

Whoever is in power affects the whole nation. Proverbs 11:11 says, **"Through the blessing of the upright a city is exalted, but by the mouth of the wicked it is destroyed."** Proverbs 29:2 adds, **"When the righteous thrive, the people rejoice; when the wicked rule, the people groan."** Proverbs 29:16 continues the thought of the importance of righteous leadership, **"When the wicked thrive, so does sin, but the righteous will see their downfall."** A key is servanthood, not political power.

The Bible is also clear on the concept of the public servant. Romans 13:4 says, **"For the one in authority is God's servant for your good. But if you do wrong, be afraid, for rulers do not bear the sword for no reason. They are God's servants, agents of wrath to bring punishment on the wrongdoer."** Authority is from God and is designed to lead through serving.

There is so much more that could be said about the godly heritage of the United States of America. Even something as simple as so many stores being closed or opening later in the day on Sunday go back to the concept taught in the Ten Commandments, **"Remember the Sabbath day by keeping it holy"** (Exodus 20:8).

Our country was founded with a Christian heritage. In 1892, the Supreme Court even said, "This is a religious people. This is a Christian nation." The Supreme Court's opening declaration for every session is, "God save the United States of America." From our currency ('In God We Trust') to swearing on a Holy Bible in the court of law, our country gives clear indicators of our beginning. We need to make sure this is not thrown out.

Does God feel comfortable in the United States?

Does He feel welcomed, needed, or wanted?

> *"If my people, who are called by my name, will humble themselves and pray and seek my face and turn from their wicked ways, then I will hear from heaven, and I will forgive their sin and will heal their land."* 2 Chronicles 7:14

09 / *Chuck Lindsey,
Reach Pastor*

BACK TO REACH

"*For Christ's love compels us, because we are convinced that one died for all, and therefore all died. And he died for all, that those who live should no longer live for themselves but for him who died for them and was raised again.*" 2 Corinthians 5:14-15 NIV

"For the Love of Christ compels me."

Why do you get out of bed each morning? Notice, I did not say "when." I said, "why do you get out of bed each morning?" If I were to ask that question to my 3-year-old daughter, she would immediately say, "to put on my dress." She wears nothing short of ball gowns nearly every day of her life. She can be regularly heard asking me if she "looks beautiful," to which I always reply, "just like your mama." It is the simplicity of a child.

What are some reasons people get up in the morning when they do not want to? _____ *adulting* _____

As adults, the answer to why we get up in the morning may not be as simple. It is a question that asks us to go beyond the surface and to honestly evaluate what drives us. It is an important question. Why do you do what you do? Is there a goal, is there a purpose, is there something you are trying to accomplish? _____

For the Apostle Paul, the goal was very simple. He could answer the question easily. Without a moment's hesitation, his answer would, no doubt, be some form of the statement: "to know Jesus and make

Him known to lost people." As you get to know him, you realize that that is sort of a summary of his life from the moment he came to Christ.

How would others summarize your life? _____
_____
_____

In the book of Acts, we see the conversion of Saul, an extremely proud man that hated Christ and Christians. He is a man that is driven by his desire to wipe out the name of Christ from the world. It is why he got up in the morning! But, just nine chapters into this great book, Saul encounters the risen Christ and is forever changed. Even his name is changed, from Saul to Paul. The Christ hater has become the Christ follower. The one who despised Christians now loves them and counts them as his true family. The change goes even deeper, for now, the mission of his life, the reason he gets up in the morning, is to see lost people saved.

Paul did not have it easy. He was told, from the very beginning, how many things he would have to suffer to bring the Gospel to lost people. A choice was put in front of him… as a choice is put in front of us all. It is God's path or our own. God's path for Paul's life would include much suffering. He suffered. But that path would also include the salvation of countless souls.

If God told you that you would suffer for sharing your faith, but that hundreds of people would be saved and in Heaven as a result of it, would you choose His path? _____
_____
_____

Why? _____
_____
_____

At the end of Paul's life, as he reflected back, he joyfully declared that though God's mission included pain and difficulty, he did not regret the course of his life. He simply said, **"Which is why I suffer as I do. But I am not ashamed, for I know whom I have believed, and I am convinced that he is able to guard until that day what has been entrusted to me"** (2 Timothy 1:12). For this reason (to bring the Gospel to lost people), Paul would suffer these things; nevertheless, he was not ashamed (he did not regret the choice to follow his path). He knew whom he had believed and was persuaded that He is able to keep what he had committed to Him until that Day. In other words, Paul said, "seeing people saved is worth whatever I had to go through!"

In 2 Corinthians 5:14 NIV, near the end of Paul's life, he simply, yet powerfully says, **"For Christ's love compels us."** When he says that, he is saying that it is Jesus' love for lost people that drives him. Think of radio, I know that might be hard in this digital age of Spotify and Apple Music. On the radio, to hear anything, you must 'tune' it to the right channel. It is all static until the dial lands on the right channel, and then the music or message comes through clearly. Our hearts are like this. Whatever channel our hearts are 'tuned' to, that is what comes through loud and clear in our lives.

What do you think it would look like if our hearts were 'tuned' to the channel of God's heart? _____
_____
_____

We do not have to guess about this. Jesus told us why He came, and why He did all He did. He said it this way, **"For the Son of Man came to seek and to save the lost"** (Luke 19:10). That was His mission. Can I tell you something? That is still His mission. It is to save lost people. If that is His mission, if that is His heart's 'radio channel,' if reaching lost people is what is 'broadcasting' from God's heart, then what happens when our heart becomes 'tuned' to His channel? That is right, it becomes our mission, too. His mission comes through loud and clear in our lives! This is why Paul said, **"For Christ's love compels us"** or drives us because the 'channel' of His heart had become tuned to the 'channel' of God's heart.

Jesus loves your lost children; He loves your lost family members, He loves your lost neighbors and co-workers. He loves them. You may be annoyed by them, but He loves them. If our hearts are tuned to His, then we will say with Paul, "it is Jesus' love for them that causes me and drives me, to get up in the morning and go to that workplace, to call that family member, to bring a pie to that neighbor, and to labor in prayer for my child."

A decision is set before you. It is set before me. It is a choice Jesus asks us both to make. Jesus said it this way, **"But seek first the kingdom of God and his righteousness, and all these things will be added to you"** (Matthew 6:33).

What are you honestly seeking 'first' (before all else)? _____
_____
_____

Why are you living? Why do you get up and do what you do? What are you trying to accomplish? 2 Corinthians 5:15 goes on to say, **"And he died for all, that those who live might no longer live for themselves but for him who for their sake died and was raised."**

Jesus died for all. Those who live (you and I) should live no longer for ourselves (what we have been used to doing, our default), but (instead) for Him who died for them and rose again.

Let Jesus' great love for lost people flood into your heart today. Ask Him to use you to reach someone, anyone, with the Gospel. When He brings that person to mind, begin to pray for them and then take a step to share the Gospel.

Take a minute to pray this to the Lord. Who has God brought to mind just now? _____
_____
_____

Every day, before your feet hit the floor, 'tune the station of your heart' and ask God to use you to share who He is with someone. He will. It is His love that drove Him and continues to drive His people.

List the names of people that God has brought to mind during this study. He wants you to begin to pray for them and then take a step to share Jesus' love with them. _____
_____
_____

TESTIMONY #1

Max Sinclair / *Children's Director*

All my life I was told that God had big and great plans for me. I grew up in the church when it was Faith Baptist; I remember the skits put on by the junior church workers. I remember the time I was saved at the age of seven. I remember making my public profession of faith with Pastor Jim and the rest of my family. Being baptized in front of the congregation of believers was something I will never forget. I remember my faith, but it was never real until now. When I graduated in 2011, I was determined not to be part of that statistic which says that most kids leave the church once they graduate high school. I was going to go to the world's largest Christian university. There is no way I could fail. I got to Liberty, and soon after, I fell. I was lost, I was scared, and I felt alone. As my father drove me home at the start of the summer break I remember seeing his face as my grades were revealed. He was so disappointed that I let him down. When they dropped me off at Liberty, they were so proud. I was the first Sinclair boy, since my grandfather, to go to college, but now I was the first to be not welcomed back. Instead of owning my mistakes and taking responsibility for my actions, I ran away. I ran to something that would make me a man. I ran to something that would give me structure to my life. I ran to the Navy.

Now besides being called to be a light in the world for Jesus, there is no higher calling than serving one's country. As I stood at attention when I was being yelled at by Recruit Divisional Commanders I remembered my calling. As I ran and endured the rigors of basic training, I remembered who I was and who I am called to be. I was called to be more than a Conqueror, and nothing on this Earth could stop me. I was going to succeed with Christ at the forefront of my life, and nothing would hold me down. Life would be difficult, but with the assurance of God in my life I would succeed because ***"No, in all these things we are more than conquerors through him who loved us"*** (Romans 8:37). With that, I did my best to be the embodiment of Honor, Courage, and Commitment with a godly mindset. I was not going to fail this time. This time I was going to live the way God calls us to live. Throughout my Naval career, I tried and I failed, but I did not run away. I knew God was calling me to do this. God was calling me to come home, do His ministry here, show His love to all, and never give up.

TESTIMONY # 2

Larry Gabbara / *Accounting Bookkeeper*

I was brought up Catholic as a child; I always knew there was a God. I went to a Catholic school through 8th grade, so that meant religious class and mass every day. I felt something missing.

As an adult, I tried to bring up my children to know God, but again still that empty feeling inside me, and I think them too. We only did it out of guilt and habit. There was not any buy in yet.

When I met and married my wife Debbie, I was living in the world. Fortunately for us, she came back to God. She then began praying for me to have an actual relationship with Jesus. This went on for 12 years. I began to go to church service with her and the kids, but still that empty feeling. The Lord was working on me; things slowly began to change. We attended a Carman concert; something happened to me that night. I knew that God was moving me.

Then there was a Power Company demonstration at the church, and I heard what salvation was that night. I still was not all in; I was only interested in a quick way to Heaven. I was not ready to put Jesus first or to build a personal relationship with Him. I was not willing to give God my whole heart. We were attending church regularly, but I was still living in the world.

My wife was still praying for me to be all in, but I was not ready. We had been talking about baptism, but I truly did not understand. Our youngest daughter accepted Jesus as her Savior and then was baptized. I did not understand it.

Proverbs 18:22 says, *"He who finds a wife finds a good thing and obtains favor from the Lord."*

I was blessed that my wife was praying diligently for my salvation.

I had heard John 3:16 (NIV), **"For God so loved the world that he gave his one and only Son, that whoever believes in him shall not perish but have eternal life."** I never actually understood the sacrifice that God made for me until that weekend.

The day that I truly was all in was a Sunday in 2002 at a Couples Conference. That weekend the Holy Spirit grabbed me. I was baptized that Sunday in Waterford, and I have been a child of God every day since.

TESTIMONY # 3

Michelle Moshier / *Nursery and Pre-K Director*

All it took was seed:
I remember as a little girl having neighbors up the road who introduced church into my life. My neighbors who have become my "second parents" took me in as if I was theirs. I did not live with them, but I did spend most of my days there. I just wanted to be away from the people in my home that made me feel unloved and unwanted. My childhood home remained broken as I grew up. Something was missing! However, God had a much bigger plan in mind.

Jeremiah 29:11 says, **"'For I know the plans I have for you,' declares the Lord 'plans to prosper you and not harm you, plans to give you hope and a future.'"** It is my belief God put that neighbor in my life to sow a seed of God's love in my heart. Unfortunately, it became buried for years as I felt alone. I thought I was not good enough for love. Something was missing! I did not feel God's presence, nor knew His best interest for me. My broken family led me toward making poor choices as I became a teenager. Such a mess! I would not change a thing. I heard the phrase, "God will never give you more than you can handle" many times not quite knowing what it meant. In 2005, my husband and I were blessed with our third son. By age two, he was diagnosed with Classic Autism. We struggled with our emotions then and still do now. God did not give us more than we can handle with His help.

In 2009, we moved to Michigan. We were searching for something! Then my life started changing. My mother-in-law and I decided to start a Bible study weekly at her home. I took this seriously. I was eagerly searching for other ways to deal with my life. During this time, I started attending church with just my children, even volunteering in the nursery. As my marriage became a struggle, the devil swooped in and stole my joy. My thoughts were that I was not worthy since I was unclean and damaged. How could God love me? I needed a drastic change. Then in October 2009, I got down on my knees in the kitchen and accepted Christ as my Lord and Savior. I was scared at first not quite knowing what it looked like to "be saved." So I took every opportunity to learn the Word of God and build a personal relationship with Him. My children and I were baptized shortly after that. My marriage was restored. Now we have been married for 14 years and attend church as a family. I did not believe that was possible. I am currently working in the children's ministry. I have always had my Protector and Comforter right by my side fighting for me. I have found I am worthy of His love. God knew what was best for me all along.

> Proverbs 3:5-6 NIV says, *"Trust in the Lord with all your heart and lean not on your own understanding; in all your ways submit to him and he will make your paths straight."*

TESTIMONY   # 4

Bill Kinney / Operations Staff

From a very young age, I went to church with my family and regularly I would hear the Gospel. I even raised my hand at the altar call several times as a young boy. Eventually, the pastor told me I only had to do it one time. My grandfather was a pastor and a true man of God. I would even help my grandparents serve food to the homeless at the Pontiac Rescue Mission. Then the teenage years came, my parents split up as many do. I started attending a church and heard stuff I did not like: how you would have to wear the right clothes and have the right haircut. I now know God does not focus on those things. That put a bad taste in my mouth about religion. I walked away from the church.

I tried to hide from God, doing all the worldly things you can think. I even road with a motorcycle club for a while. It was a very hard life. I went from job to job and even state to state trying to find what was missing in my life.

Now after a lot of wasted years (like 25 or so) of running and trying to hide from God, I kept hearing God call me. Once I answered God's call, I started to change. This time I could feel the Holy Spirit in me. All I wanted to do was please my Heavenly Father. I now know what that pastor meant that you only need to ask the Lord to be your Savior and Lord of your life one time. It is a relationship with God. He enters you. You can feel Him in every part of your life! All I know now is serving the Lord is all I want to do for the rest of my time in this world. It is way better than any worldly thing you can imagine.

Ephesians 2:10 is one of my favorite verses, **"For we are his workmanship, created in Christ Jesus for good works, which God prepared beforehand, that we should walk in them."**

TESTIMONY   # 5

James Mann / *Children's Director*

I was born into a Christian home and lived a cookie-cutter Christian childhood. I was saved at the age of five, and I was baptized, at Faith Baptist, later that year. I was the child that could tell you everything about the Bible and recite countless verses that were learned in Awana. When I was nine years old, my life flipped upside down. My parents got a divorce. My dad ended up moving to Florida to work with my Grandpa. I was bitter and angry, not only with my parents but with God as well. How could God do this to me? Was I not doing everything He told me to do? This began my downward spiral away from Him.

My parents only stayed separated for one year. They ended up remarrying each other, and my mom and I moved to Florida to join him. Florida was the furthest I have ever felt from God in my entire life. We tried to find a church that we could call home, but after many attempts, we just gave up. This was when I started living completely in the world. I was not doing anything too crazy, but it was not what God intended for my life. Florida was the most difficult six years of my life. My Grandpa ended up passing away, and our family realized there was nothing left for us in Florida. We packed everything up and headed home to Michigan.

Once we got here, we began to attend church almost immediately. We went to The River Church. I was hesitant from the beginning. I fought with my parents for six months. They wanted me to join the youth group, and I did everything possible to get out of it. Finally, the Student Pastor at the time contacted my mom and said they were going on a leadership retreat. My mom just mentioned it to me but did not say anymore. I did not know what it was, but something inside me told me to go. So, I asked my mom if I could go. That was my first time doing something with the church in nine years. My life changed at that moment. At the age of 17, I decided that I was done living the way I was, and it was time to get back on track. It was not an easy transition. God challenged me in many ways and forced me to lean on Him. He performed many miracles in my life. I realized that if He was not in control that I would have died before the age of 18. It was at this point that I decided to jump completely into this new lifestyle. I wanted to join the ministry field. That is when I fell in love with children's ministry. He made it clear to me that I am meant to be a Children's Pastor someday, so that is the path I decided to follow and I love every second of it.

TESTIMONY # 6

Richie Henson / *Production Director*

Growing up in the church as the son of a pastor, it became easy for me to do the right thing in front of the right people. I spent much of my time presenting a Christian facade while struggling with depression and anger on the inside. During my high school years, this reality became exceedingly difficult to maintain. I struggled with keeping it all together, and I knew that my current situation was not sustainable. June of 2013, while at Ponderosa Pines summer camp, the speaker began to talk about the importance of putting your faith in Jesus and that it is not enough to rely on your good choices and actions. I began to realize during this week that I had never really made a choice to follow Jesus. I had never made a conscious decision to put my faith in Jesus as my Lord and Savior.

On Thursday night, the topic of feeling overwhelmed came up. This resonated with me so deeply, and I knew God was reaching out to me. I felt that the world was overcoming me at every turn and I could not see a way out, but Jesus was offering me a way out. Jesus was offering me grace and salvation that could radically change me and make me a conqueror in a fallen world.

> 1 John 5:5 says,
> *"Who is it that overcomes the world except the one who believes that Jesus is the Son of God?"*

My whole life had been about creating perceptions that would not let people know I was broken and overwhelmed. I broke down and sought help and guidance to accept Jesus as my Savior. From that point, my life was transformed as I began to see life and the world through the perspective of victory in Jesus. I was finally able to release my insecurities and anger as I grew in true community with other believers for the first time.

The world is a rough place. It is full of sin and disappointment, but Jesus' saving grace provides us with the opportunity to walk in freedom as conquerors.

TESTIMONY   # 7

Ben Heddy-Kennedy / *Operations Staff*

I was raised in a close-knit family. Growing up we did a lot together, but the church was not one of those things. My uncle is a music director at a church, so we attended his church on special holidays, but that was about it. Things changed when I started middle school. A friend invited my sisters, a couple of other friends, and me to The River Church (Goodrich) all-nighter. It sounded like fun, so we all went. Sometime in the middle of all the craziness, the youth director got up and spoke about Hell, Heaven, and Jesus. I raised my hand, met with him, and repeated a prayer he said. I do not think it sunk in at that point. I believe that was a turning point for our family. My parents rededicated their lives, our whole family started going to church together, and I attended both Sunday and Thursday youth group times.

Ninth grade is a transition time for all kids, but it was a real tough time for me. I felt alone and even depressed. I got serious about reading the Bible and prayer. It was then that I got serious about following Christ. I tend to be on the shy side and hang out behind the scenes, but I knew I was not alone. The youth core group Bible studies and 5th quarter became part of my routine. That middle school prayer now made more sense.

My favorite verses are 1 Thessalonians 4:11-12, **"And to aspire to live quietly, and to mind your own affairs, and to work with your hands, as we instructed you, so that you may walk properly before outsiders and be dependent on no one."** I recently saw these verses and felt they dictated my view on life. We need to be people known for working hard. It is important to get down to it and get it done. I take a healthy pride in being part of the Operations Staff at Church. Recently, when I was setting up chairs for a concert,

I thought about how I was doing something important and all the people that would now have a place to sit comfortably. I must admit, bathrooms are not my favorite, but I make sure people can trust they are clean. I know what I do makes a difference for others and eventually even the Gospel.

We are all part of the Body of Christ, and each one of us needs to be diligent in what the Lord has for us.

OUR MISSION

Matthew 28:19-20: *"Go therefore and make disciples of all nations, baptizing them in the name of the Father and of the Son and of the Holy Spirit, teaching them to observe all that I have commanded you. And behold, I am with you always, to the end of the age."*

REACH

At The River Church, you will often hear the phrase, "we don't go to church, we are the Church." We believe that as God's people, our primary purpose and goal is to go out and make disciples of Jesus Christ. We encourage you to reach the world in your local communities.

GATHER

Weekend Gatherings at The River Church are all about Jesus, through singing, giving, serving, baptizing, taking the Lord's Supper, and participating in messages that are all about Jesus and bringing glory to Him. We know that when followers of Christ gather together in unity, it's not only a refresher it's bringing life-change.

GROW

Our Growth Communities are designed to mirror the early church in Acts as having "all things in common." They are smaller collections of believers who spend time together studying the word, knowing and caring for one another relationally, and learning to increase their commitment to Christ by holding one another accountable.

The River Church
8393 E. Holly Rd. Holly, MI 48442
theriverchurch.cc • info@theriverchurch.cc

BOOKS BY THE RIVER CHURCH

Made in the USA
Columbia, SC
21 November 2017